Aspects of Ch … ity

Christian Life

MICHAEL KEENE

Stanley Thornes (Publishers) Ltd

First published in 2000 by:
Stanley Thornes (Publishers) Ltd
Delta Place
27 Bath Road
CHELTENHAM GL53 7TH
England

00 01 02 03 04 / 10 9 8 7 6 5 4 3 2 1

A catalogue record for this book is available from the British Library.

ISBN 0-7487-5287-0

Printed and bound in China by Dah Hua Printing Press Co. Ltd.

Page layout by Penny and Tony Mills
Illustrated by Richard Johnson

Acknowledgements

With thanks to the following for permission to reproduce photographs and other copyright material in this book:

Alex Keene for all photographs.

Scriptures quoted from the *Good News Bible* published by The Bible Societies/HarperCollins Publishers Ltd., UK, © American Bible Society, 1966, 1971, 1976, 1992.

Every effort has been made to contact copyright holders. The publishers apologise to anyone whose rights have been inadvertently overlooked, and will be happy to rectify any errors or omissions.

Note: Throughout the series BCE (Before Common or Christian Era) and CE (Common or Christian Era) have been used in place of the traditional BC and AD. The new terms are more acceptable to followers of non-Christian religions.

CONTENTS

1 Christian worship

Christians and worship 4
Cathedrals 6
Churches (1) 8
Churches (2) 10
Prayer (1) 12
Prayer (2) 14
Using the Bible (1) 16
Using the Bible (2) 18

2 People and events

Bishops, priests and ministers 20
Monks and nuns 22
The Sacraments 24
Holy Communion 26
Infant baptism 28
Confirmation 30
Believer's baptism 32
Seeking forgiveness 34
Marriage 36
Death 38
Symbols 40
Music 42

3 Celebrations

The Christian year 44
Advent 46
Christmas 48
Lent 50
Palm Sunday 52
Maundy Thursday 54
Good Friday 56
Easter Day 58
Ascension Day and Pentecost 60

4 Christian beliefs

The Creeds 62
The Trinity 64
God, the Father 66
Jesus, God's Son 68
The Death and Resurrection of Jesus 70
The Holy Spirit 72
The Virgin Mary 74

Glossary **76**

1 Christian worship

CHRISTIANS AND WORSHIP

- **Sunday is the main day on which Christians meet together to worship God.**
- **Many churches use a prayer book which contains the words of the main services.**
- **Other churches do not use a prayer book and their services mainly involve singing, praying, reading from the Bible and a sermon.**

Christians meet regularly to worship God and pray with each other. Usually they do this in a church but they can also meet in each other's homes to worship. In some churches the worship is quiet and thoughtful. Part of the service may be spent in total silence so that people can listen to their own thoughts about God. Other services are much noisier with loud music, dancing and clapping. Christians can choose which kind of service they prefer to attend. People are very different in their tastes and Christians are no exception.

Two kinds of worship

You can divide Christian worship into two different approaches:

a Churches which use a prayer book, containing the services which people can follow. The services in most Anglican (Church of England) and Roman Catholic churches are like this. Anglicans use the old Book of Common Prayer or the modern Alternative Services Book whilst Roman Catholic services are found in the Missal. Hymns, chanting (a special kind of singing), prayers, Bible readings and a sermon make up the worship.

b Churches which do not have a set service. Nonconformist Churches, such as Methodist and Baptist, have services which depend heavily upon singing, personal testimonies, praying and preaching.

A *Why has this group of Christians come together to worship God?*

B *You can see at least two symbols in this act of worship. Describe them and find out a little about them.*

A special day

Sunday is the main day when Christians come together to worship God. This day, often called 'The Lord's Day', was adopted by Christians in the fourth century since Jesus rose from the dead on the first day of the week. With the change in the Sunday laws in this country in the 1990s many Christians find that they now have to work on Sundays. To meet the needs of all people services are held in most churches on other days of the week as well. If possible, though, most Christians still try to find some time to worship with other believers in church on Sunday.

Why worship?

Worship is a very important part of the Christian life. Christians find that it gives them the opportunity:

a To express their deepest feelings for God – whether praise, thanksgiving, wonder or love. Different people wish to express these feelings in different ways. This is why church services are very different. Praying, singing, reflecting, clapping and incense-burning are all part of Christian worship for different people.

b To find God's forgiveness for themselves and to forgive others who have hurt them.

c To be inspired through meeting with other Christians and to find strength to serve God in their daily lives.

d To celebrate the main events in the life of Jesus.

IN THE GLOSSARY

Anglican Church; Bible; Church of England; Nonconformist Church; Roman Catholic Church; Sermon; Sunday.

WHAT DO YOU KNOW?

1 a On which day of the week do Christians try to meet together to praise God?

b What are the names of two prayer books used by Anglicans?

c What is the name of the prayer book used by Roman Catholics?

d Which group of Churches does not use a prayer book?

e List three ingredients that you would expect to find in most Christian acts of worship?

2 What do you think are the main advantages of having:

i services in a prayer book which everyone can follow?

ii services which take a different form week by week?

3 You have the opportunity of designing a church service that would appeal to yourself and your friends. What would you want it to contain?

1 Christian worship

CATHEDRALS

- **Bishops in the Anglican and Roman Catholic Churches preside over a cathedral.**
- **Each cathedral is identified by having a 'bishop's seat'.**
- **Built centuries ago, most cathedrals provided the opportunity for craftsmen to use their skills in the worship of God.**

Cathedrals are special church buildings. The Anglican and Roman Catholic Churches divide the country up into areas, called dioceses. Each diocese is led by a bishop, a senior priest, and the church of the bishop is the cathedral. When the great cathedrals (bishop's seats) were built bishops were wealthy landowners and, sometimes, the cathedral was built in their honour. In other areas, though, the most beautiful or largest church in the diocese became the cathedral.

A What do you think a person might gain from attending a service in a cathedral?

The bishop's seat

Each cathedral has a large chair, often beautifully carved in wood. This is the chair of the bishop and he sits on it when he conducts a service in the cathedral. This practice goes back centuries to the time when the bishop always sat directly behind the altar. This is where you will still find the bishop's seat in a cathedral.

Cathedral buildings

Most cathedrals are large, magnificent and awe-inspiring (see pictures A and B). When most of them were built centuries ago they provided opportunities for craftsmen to use their considerable skills to build a monument to the glory of God. For many of them building a cathedral was their lifetime's work. In some cases the monument has lasted for almost a thousand years.

The long passage-way (the nave) down the centre of the cathedral was often used in previous ages by traders to sell their goods. It provided them with a shelter in which they could work in all weathers. No one considered this to be a degrading use for a 'House of God' although it soon became apparent that such

B How would you describe the interior of a cathedral to someone who had never been in one?

activity could interfere with the main purpose of the building – the worship of God. To separate business from worship a screen was erected at the front of the cathedral to keep the altar area holy. This screen was called a 'rood screen' because it often contained a 'rood' (a cross) in its design. The cross is the main symbol of the Christian religion because of its link with the death of Jesus.

Most of these rood screens have long since been removed from cathedrals. Today people want to be as close as possible to the altar as they worship God. New cathedrals, such as those in Liverpool (Anglican and Roman Catholic) and Bristol (Roman Catholic), are round or semi-circular rather than cross-like in shape. This allows people to feel closely involved in the worship since, wherever they are sitting, they are not far from the altar.

There are many services each Sunday and, usually, other services during the week in a cathedral. Some of these services are taken by the bishop but he is also expected to take services elsewhere in his diocese. Cathedrals are also used for special services when people travel from all over the diocese to attend. Important national occasions such as a royal wedding or a funeral are often held in cathedrals.

IN THE GLOSSARY

Altar; Anglican Church; Bishop; Cathedral; Diocese; Nave; Roman Catholic Church; Rood screen; Sunday.

WHAT DO YOU KNOW?

1 a What does the word 'cathedral' mean?
b What is a bishop?
c What is the 'bishop's seat'?
d Where will you find the 'bishop's seat' in a cathedral?
e What is a 'rood screen'?

2 Why do you think that craftsmen in the past wanted to be able to use their skills for the glory of God?

3 Look at photographs A and B. What do you think there is in a cathedral which might help to direct a person's thoughts to God?

1 Christian worship

CHURCHES (1)

- **Most of the churches in Great Britain belong to the Church of England.**
- **Church of England and Roman Catholic churches have priests who take most of the services.**
- **Nonconformist churches, such as Baptist and Methodist, are usually much smaller and are led by ministers.**

There are thousands of churches in England and Wales belonging to the different denominations. Almost half of them belong to the Church of England and about a million people attend them regularly for worship. A similar number of people go to Roman Catholic churches although there are far fewer of them. Thousands more worship in smaller churches or chapels (called Nonconformist churches) such as Baptist, Methodist and Salvation Army.

A Write down five words that come into your mind as you look at this photograph of a church.

The Church of England

Church of England churches are also called 'parish churches'. Each diocese in the Church of England is divided up into 'parishes'. This is the area around a church from which most of its congregation come. A parish church has a priest (vicar) and the larger of them also have assistant priests (curates). In country areas, though, a vicar may have more than one church to look after.

The vicar takes most of the services in his church and also visits church members in their homes, especially if they are sick. Many parish churches are very old although others have been built recently on new housing estates. Even people who do not go to church may have a link with their parish church by being baptised and married there. They will probably also be buried there. The parish church is an important part of the local community.

The Roman Catholic Church

From the outside Church of England and Roman Catholic buildings look similar. Inside, though, there are differences. Inside a Roman Catholic church you

B For many people their parish church is a very important part of their lives. Why do you think this is?

will see many crucifixes and a statue of the Virgin Mary but you will only see these in a few Church of England churches. You can find out more about the Virgin Mary on pages 74–5.

Orthodox churches

There are only a few Orthodox churches in this country although there are thousands of them elsewhere in Europe. The dome of an Orthodox church reminds worshippers of the heavens that have been stretched by God over the earth. The square shape of the building is a reminder that everyone is equal in God's sight. The four corners of the building show that people are drawn from all parts of the earth to worship God.

Nonconformist churches

There are many churches which are called 'Nonconformist'. They were built from the seventeenth century onwards and include Baptist, Methodist, United Reformed, Salvation Army and Quaker places of worship amongst others. Most of these buildings, often called 'chapels', are small and rather plain inside. Members of the Salvation Army call their religious buildings 'citadels' whilst Quakers gather for worship in 'Meeting houses'.

IN THE GLOSSARY

Baptist Church; Church of England; Citadel; Crucifix; Curate; Diocese; Meeting house; Methodist Church; Nonconformist Church; Orthodox Church; Priest; Quakers; Roman Catholic Church; Salvation Army; United Reformed Church; Vicar; Virgin Mary.

WHAT DO YOU KNOW?

1 a What is a parish church?
b What are vicars and curates?
c How do many people come into contact with their parish church?
d Which two objects are always found in a Roman Catholic church?
e What are Salvation Army and Quaker places of worship called?

2 Why do you think that the most important events in a person's life often centre around church – even though they may not attend church at any other time?

3 Do you think it is surprising that fewer and fewer people are regularly attending church? How do you think churches might attract more people?

1 Christian worship

CHURCHES (2)

- **For many Christians the building in which they worship God is very important.**
- **The altar is the focal-point of Anglican, Roman Catholic and Orthodox churches.**
- **The font and the pulpit play important roles in many church services.**

Some Christians do not think that the place in which they worship God is particularly important. They are just as happy worshipping in a community hall or someone's home as in a church.

A *Where would you be likely to find this font in a church? Why?*

Others – like the Plymouth Brethren and the Quakers – deliberately keep their places of worship as simple, and as plain, as possible. They argue that nothing should distract them during worship. The majority of Christians, however, love the place in which they meet with other Christians to worship God. To them it is a holy place with an atmosphere of its own which makes them aware of God's presence.

Places of worship

Christian churches vary a great deal but most of them do have some features in common:

a The altar. In Anglican, Roman Catholic and Orthodox churches the altar is the holiest part of the church. In most churches it stands in front of the east wall. As the priest conducts the Eucharist or Holy Communion he or she stands behind the altar facing the people. People worship facing east towards the altar since this is where the sun rises. For centuries Christians have taken the rising sun to be a symbol of the resurrection of Jesus from the dead.

b The pulpit. Most churches have a pulpit. In Nonconformist churches it is the focal-point of the church. The priest or minister preaches the sermon during the service from the pulpit. The pulpit is a platform which raises the priest above the people so

B Why are candles an important feature in many churches?

that everyone can see and hear what he or she is saying.

c The font. Anglican, Roman Catholic and Orthodox buildings have a font (see picture A) which usually stands just inside the door of the church. The font is a stone or wooden bowl which holds the water used during the service of infant baptism. Its position in a church reminds people that infant baptism is the 'door' through which a child passes to become a member of the church.

d Stained-glass windows. Stained-glass windows are a feature of many churches. In the days before many people could read or write stained-glass windows were used to teach them stories from the Bible or about the lives of the saints. They were an early, and important, teaching-aid.

The shape of many of the older churches was important. The central aisle down the middle (the nave) was crossed by another aisle in front of the sanctuary to form a cross-shape. The shape of the church is a reminder to everyone of the death of Jesus. The people sit on either side of the aisle in pews. Candles are a feature of many churches (see picture B) although they are not found in Nonconformist churches. People often light a candle before they say a prayer – the candles used for this purpose are called 'votive candles'. Candles remind worshippers of Jesus who described himself as 'the Light of the world'.

IN THE GLOSSARY

Altar; Anglican Church; Bible; Eucharist; Holy Communion; Infant baptism; Jerusalem; Orthodox Church; Pulpit; Quakers; Roman Catholic Church; Saint.

WHAT DO YOU KNOW?

1 a Name one Christian group which keeps its places of worship as simple as possible.
b Why is this important to them?
c Why is the altar placed in front of the east wall in most churches?
d What happens in the pulpit during a service?
e What is the font used for?

2 Why do you think that many Christians prefer to worship God in a plain and simple building?

3 Churches are full of symbolism. How do you think that symbols help people to worship in church?

1 Christian worship

PRAYER (1)

- **Prayer is very important to Christians. They sometimes pray on their own and sometimes with others.**
- **Praise, confession, petition and intercession are all very important ingredients of Christian prayer.**
- **Jesus gave the Lord's Prayer to his disciples as a model for their own prayers.**

When Christians pray they are talking to God but they also listen to God speaking to them. To hear God they try to empty their minds of all distracting thoughts. Prayer is often a group activity – in church or in someone's house. Sometimes the leader says a prayer and the people join in at the end by saying 'Amen' (So be it, Lord). If the people are following a service in a prayer book then everyone joins in and says the prayer together.

Prayer is also a private activity. Many Christians say their own prayers on waking up in the morning and before going to sleep at night. Many say a prayer of thankfulness before or after eating a meal (called the 'grace'). Christians often pray before making an important decision or facing up to a big challenge.

Kinds of prayer

There are many different kinds of prayer that Christians use:

a **Praise**. This is a prayer of thankfulness to God for his beautiful creation and for the gift of life. It also recognises how great God is.

b **Confession**. This is the feeling that, faced with God's greatness, the only response is to be aware of one's own sinfulness. In the Roman Catholic Church worshippers are encouraged to confess their sins to God through a priest and to receive the promise of God's forgiveness (the 'absolution'). In other churches people are encouraged to ask for God's forgiveness in all of their prayers.

c **Petition**. A prayer in which a worshipper asks God to help them with particular matters which are bothering them.

A *Do you think that children can, or should, be taught how to pray?*

B People often kneel as they pray. Why do you think this symbolic action is important to them?

d Intercession. These are prayers which are offered up for other people. Christians pray for the lonely, the hungry, the poor and the needy people in the world.

Meditation is a slightly different way of praying. Whilst most prayers are spoken out loud meditation is a silent way of praying in which the worshipper concentrates his or her mind on God. This way of praying has been used for centuries by monks and nuns but it has now become more popular amongst Christians generally. Many use it as a way of relaxing in the middle of a busy and hectic life.

The Lord's Prayer

There is only one Christian prayer which is used by worshippers of every Church. This is the prayer which begins 'Our Father, who art in heaven' and is called the Lord's Prayer or 'Our Father' by many Roman Catholics. This prayer is treasured by Christians above all others because it is the prayer that Jesus taught his own disciples to use.

IN THE GLOSSARY

Absolution; Lord's Prayer; Meditation; Monk; Nun; Prayer book; Priest; Roman Catholic Church.

WHAT DO YOU KNOW?

1 a What do Christians say at the end of all their prayers and what does it mean?
b What kind of prayer is the 'grace'?
c Which Church encourages its members to seek God's forgiveness for their sins through the priest?
d What is the 'absolution'?
e What is the difference between petition and intercession?

2 Why do you think many Christians find that meditation is a difficult form of prayer to use?

3 The Lord's Prayer is often taken by Christians to be a symbol of their unity with each other even though they may have differences. Why do you think this is?

1 Christian worship

PRAYER (2)

- **A rosary is a string of beads which reminds a worshipper of special prayers and events in the life of Jesus.**
- **Icons are special religious paintings which are earthly copies of heavenly images.**
- **Icons are an important feature of Orthodox buildings and candles are often lit in front of them as an act of worship.**

Many Christians believe that they can talk to God directly without any help. Others, though, find that prayer is a very difficult business. In some churches help is provided in one of two ways:

1 **The rosary**. The rosary (see picture A) is a string of beads which a person holds between their fingers. There are 50 beads on the rosary and these are arranged in five groups with single beads separating the groups of ten. There is a crucifix at the end of the string. In passing the beads through their fingers a worshipper is reminded of:

a Three important prayers. The Lord's Prayer, the Hail Mary (the Ave Maria) and the Gloria Patri. The 'Hail Mary' is a prayer to the Virgin Mary in which her help is sought by the worshipper. The 'Gloria Patri' gives glory to God the Father, God the Son and God the Holy Spirit – the three members of the Godhead known as the 'Trinity'.

b Fifteen important 'mysteries' in the Christian faith – the 'joyful mysteries', the 'sorrowful mysteries' and the 'glorious mysteries'. This takes the worshipper from the birth and life of Jesus, through his death on a cross to his resurrection and the journey of Mary into heaven at the end of her life. Each person thinks deeply about just one of these mysteries whilst using the rosary.

2 **Icons**. Icons (see picture B) are an important part of worship in an Orthodox family and church. They are special religious paintings which are used by worshippers to help them pray. The paintings may be of Mary with or without the baby Jesus, Jesus

A Find out what the word 'rosary' means.

B Describe what you see in this icon. What makes it different from any other painting?

himself, the Holy Family of Mary, Joseph and Jesus, an apostle or one of the saints of the Church.

Icons are not like any other paintings. They can only be produced by Orthodox painters who have been specially trained. Before they begin painting artists must spend time praying, fasting and spiritually preparing themselves. Each icon is a copy of a perfect image which exists in heaven. They are usually painted in bright colours on wood although other materials can be used. Worshippers light a candle in front of one of them as they enter to worship.

Icons are kept by Orthodox people in their home as well as in church. In church they are placed on the walls There is also an important screen which separates the High Altar from the people in the congregation called the iconostasis. The Royal Doors in the middle of the iconostasis are opened to allow the priest to pass through at important times in the service of the Holy Liturgy. There are two icons on either side of the Royal doors – one showing the birth of Jesus and the other the return of Jesus to the earth.

IN THE GLOSSARY

Apostle; Crucifix; Hail Mary; Holy Liturgy; Icon; Iconostasis; Lord's Prayer; Priest; Rosary; Royal doors; Saint; Trinity; Virgin Mary.

WHAT DO YOU KNOW?

1 a Which three prayers is the Roman Catholic worshipper reminded of by the rosary?

b How many 'mysteries' are there on the rosary?

c In which church are you most likely to find an icon?

d Which figures might be included on a rosary?

e What is the iconostasis and what is on it?

2 Why do you think the Orthodox Church looks upon the painting of icons as very important spiritual work in itself which must be preceded by prayer and fasting?

3 Candles play a very important part in Christian worship. Find out two other ways in which candles are used in church.

USING THE BIBLE (1)

- **The Bible plays a very important part in the lives of most Christians.**
- **The Bible is used for private study as well as in public worship.**
- **Christians believe that God speaks to them through the Bible through the guidance of the Holy Spirit.**

The Bible stands at the heart of the Christian faith and plays a very important part in worship, both public and private. The Bible is divided into two parts – the Old Testament and the New Testament.

A Do you think it is helpful to have a guide to help you through life?

The 39 books of the Old Testament form the Jewish Sacred Scriptures although the books are in a different order. Jesus and his disciples were all Jews who were very familiar with their Scriptures.

The New Testament is concerned with Jesus, the Messiah, whose coming into the world was prophesied in the Old Testament. The New Testament contains two main kinds of writings:

a **History**. This includes four Gospels – Matthew, Mark, Luke and John – which describe the life and teachings of Jesus. The first three have a similar way of presenting their material and are called the Synoptic ('looking together') Gospels. The Acts of the Apostles, which follows these four Gospels, describes the early history of the Christian Church after Jesus left the earth.

b **Letters or Epistles.** There are many letters in the New Testament written to guide and help early Christian believers. Most of them were written by Paul but others came from Peter and John, amongst others.

Using the Bible

The Bible plays a very important part in the lives of individual Christians as well as being used widely in Christian worship (see next unit). Many Christians set aside a time each day during which they pray and read the Bible (see picture A). They might call this their

'Quiet Time'. Christians do this at a time which fits in best with their own personal lifestyle. For some it might be in the morning before they go to work or in the evening when work is finished.

Many Christians believe that God speaks to them through the Bible. They spend some time praying before they read to seek God's guidance through the Holy Spirit. Many parts of the Bible are not easy to understand. Studying the background to the different books may help the reader to make sense of what they are reading. To help people further Bible-study notes are available which take a reader through the whole Bible in three to five years. There are different notes which are tailored to meet the needs of children, young people and adults.

Sometimes Christians meet together to study a passage from the Bible (see picture B). In many churches this happens regularly. In Anglican and Roman Catholic churches it is most likely to happen during Lent as church members prepare themselves for the festival of Easter. During this season they spend time reading and praying about the death and resurrection of Jesus to try to understand more about the events which are at the heart of their Christian faith.

B Why do you think many Christians come together regularly to study the Bible?

IN THE GLOSSARY

Anglican Church; Bible; Easter; Epistle; Gospel; Holy Spirit; Lent; Messiah; New Testament; Old Testament; Paul; Peter; Roman Catholic Church; Synoptic Gospels.

WHAT DO YOU KNOW?

1 a Into which two parts is the Bible divided?
b Into which two parts is the New Testament divided?
c What is 'Quiet Time'?
d What help is available for a Christian trying to understand the Bible?
e During which season of the year are Christians most likely to meet to study the Bible. Why?

2 Imagine that you are a Christian who is fairly new to reading the Bible. What might you hope to gain from it?

3 What do you think are the main advantages, and problems, of regularly reading the Bible?

1 Christian worship

USING THE BIBLE (2)

- **In most church services there are three readings from the Bible taken from the Old Testament, the Epistles and the Gospels.**
- **Whilst the readings from the Old Testament and the Epistles can be taken by a lay-person the one from the Gospels is usually read by the priest.**
- **The sermon, an important part of a Nonconformist service, is an opportunity to explain a passage from the Bible and its relevance to people today.**

The Bible was put together over a long period of time to provide inspiration, and teaching, for those who belonged to the Christian community. The Church draws constantly on the inspiration that it provides. The Bible is used in almost all church services – passages are read from it and sermons are based on its teaching.

A Why do Christians believe that it is important to know the Bible?

Reading the Bible in church

In the Church of England and the Roman Catholic Church most services include three readings from the Bible:

- an Old Testament reading.
- a reading from the Epistles.
- a reading from the Gospels.

The readings from the Old Testament and the Epistles can be read, and usually are, by an ordinary member of the congregation. Such a person is called a 'lay-person'. In the last 30 years both Churches have made much greater use of ordinary church members in the planning and leading of their worship. Both of these readings are given from the lectern positioned to one side of the chancel and altar. The lectern often has an eagle on the front. In Roman Catholic and Orthodox churches the Gospel reading is taken by the priest. Often the Gospel is carried above the heads of the servers into the nave of the church where it is read to the people. This underlines the Christian belief that, whilst all of the Bible is inspired by God in some way, the Gospels carry a special authority. They contain all that we know about the life and teaching of Jesus, the Son of God. Obviously his teaching carries an authority that cannot be found elsewhere in the Bible.

B How do church services help Christians to know the Bible better?

The people listen very carefully to the Gospel reading in case God speaks to them through it.

The sermon

The preaching about the Bible during a sermon by the priest, or someone else authorised to do so, is very important in Nonconformist churches. In these churches people usually bring a Bible with them to church because the sermon is the time when they hope that God will speak to them. Many of them actually refer to the Bible as 'God's Word'. The sermon is also an important part of worship in an Anglican church whilst in Roman Catholic churches it is called a 'homily' rather than a sermon. People not only come to church to worship God but also to find out more about the Christian life. The sermon is the main way to learn about this. Christians are then encouraged to go out into the world to serve God and to put the teachings of the Bible into practice.

IN THE GLOSSARY

Altar; Anglican Church; Bible; Church of England; Epistles; Gospel; Lectern; Nonconformist Church; Old Testament; Orthodox Church; Priest; Roman Catholic Church; Sermon.

WHAT DO YOU KNOW?

1 a Who usually reads from the Old Testament and the Epistles, in the New Testament, during a service?
b Where do most of the readings from the Bible take place during a service?
c How is the Gospel reading treated differently from the other Bible readings in many church services?
d Why is the Gospel reading treated differently from the other readings in a service?
e What is a sermon?

2 Imagine that you are in a church service and you listen to three readings from the Bible. What do you think you are intended to understand by the fact that the Gospel reading is treated differently from the others?

3 Someone has said that the sermon has become an out-of-date way of teaching about the Christian faith. Do you agree with this comment? Can you think of a better way to teach religious truth?

2 People *and* events

BISHOPS, PRIESTS AND MINISTERS

- **Most Churches have priests or ministers who are responsible for leading the people in their worship.**
- **Priests are ordained by the bishop in a special service at the beginning of their ministry.**
- **Being ordained gives priests the authority to give the sacraments to members of their congregation.**

Not all of the Christian Churches have full-time, professional leaders. Some, like the Quakers, prefer to elect their leader from members of the congregation. This person is an unpaid secretary who organises the services and other activities in the Meeting house. The Roman Catholic, Anglican and Orthodox Churches have priests (see picture A) although only the Anglican Church allows women to be priests. A person who is a priest, male or female, is said to be in Holy Orders. All of these Churches have senior priests who are bishops. Nonconformist churches have ministers (see picture B) who lead the worship in their churches but the Salvation Army has officers who wear a distinctive uniform.

Leaders

In the Roman Catholic Church the Pope, who is the Bishop of Rome, is the supreme leader. Roman Catholics believe that the Pope, and his bishops, are the direct successors of the first disciples of Jesus. They inherit the power and authority which Jesus gave to the apostles. The Anglican Church is a collection of Churches, in different countries, that follows the leadership of the Church of England and the Archbishop of Canterbury. There are many different Orthodox churches and each one of them is led by its own Patriarch (Archbishop).

A *Find out what the word 'priest' means.*

B *Why do Nonconformist churches call their leaders 'ministers'?*

Priests

After training each priest is 'ordained' to the priesthood. At their ordination the bishop lays his hands on their head and asks for God's blessing on their future ministry. He also gives them authority to give the sacraments to members of their churches. This is considered to be the most important part of a priest's work. Roman Catholic priests take a vow of 'celibacy' which means that they promise not to marry whilst they are in the priesthood.

Ministers

Nonconformist churches usually have their own minister. He or she is responsible for taking most of the services in the church although they are also expected to visit other churches from time to time. As their name suggests these people are expected to 'minister' spiritually to church members just as Jesus did to his disciples. Most Nonconformist churches have regular Breaking of Bread services (Holy Communion) as well as baptising either children or adults. Although these services can be conducted by ordinary members of the congregation they are usually led by the minister.

IN THE GLOSSARY

Anglican Church; Bishop; Bishop of Rome; Breaking of Bread; Celibacy; Holy Communion; Holy Orders; Meeting house; Minister; Nonconformist Church; Ordination; Orthodox Church; Pope; Priest; Quakers; Roman Catholic Church; Sacrament; Salvation Army.

WHAT DO YOU KNOW?

1 a Which is the only Christian Church to allow female priests?

b What are Holy Orders?

c Who is the Bishop of Rome?

d Who do Roman Catholics believe to be the successors of the disciples of Jesus?

e What is ordination?

2 What do you think might be the advantages and disadvantages of having full-time leaders of a Christian community?

3 Why do you think a bishop lays his hands on the head of someone who is to become a priest?

2 People *and* events

MONKS AND NUNS

- **Monks and nuns are people who have chosen to dedicate their lives to God**
- **Monks and nuns believe that they have a 'vocation' (calling) to live in a religious community.**
- **Each monk and nun takes a three-fold vow of poverty, chastity and obedience.**

Monks and nuns are men and women who have chosen to dedicate their lives to God and his service. Almost from the beginning of the Christian faith there were people who chose to live in the desert, following the example of Jesus, to pray. To begin with these people were hermits, living on their own, but they soon started to live in communities with their own rules. Today there are still thousands of monks and nuns – mainly in the Roman Catholic and Orthodox Churches. Their number, though, is far fewer than it was a few years ago.

A *Why did early monks go into the desert?*

Religious Orders

Monks and nuns live together in communities – monks in monasteries and nuns in convents. Each of them believes that they have a 'vocation' (calling) from God to live in this way. Each community belongs to a Religious Order – the Carmelites, the Benedictines, the Augustinians, etc. Although each Religious Order has its own rules they all live by 'the Rule' which goes all the way back to St Benedict in the fifth century. This Rule has three vows which each new member of the Order takes:

a **The Vow of Poverty**. Each person entering a Religious Order tries to live as closely as possible to the example of Jesus. Jesus lived a life of poverty without having any material possessions of his own. The Christian disciple is called by God to live in the same way. On joining a community a person hands over all of their possessions to be used for the good of others. The community then provides them with all that they need.

b **The Vow of Chastity**. Monks and nuns are not allowed to marry. They are not allowed to form any

B *Do you think monks and nuns could work amongst the really poor if they hadn't taken a vow of poverty?*

close relationships. Instead, on entering the monastery or convent they become 'married' to God. Anything else would be a distraction.

c The Vow of Obedience. In a monastery the leader of the community is the Abbot whilst in a convent it is the Mother Superior. In most communities the leader is elected by members of the community. The will of God and of the community is expressed by its leader and so that person is to be obeyed without question.

By living their life by these three vows each monk and nun is free to serve God at all times. The most important duty of everyone in the community is that of prayer. In the traditional monasteries and convents prayer is offered seven times a day – starting from the early morning and finishing in the early evening. In modern communities, though, the number of times that people come together to pray is reduced.

Some religious communities are 'closed' and their members only have very limited contact with the outside world. In closed communities praying is the 'work' that God has called the men or women to perform. In other communities, however, there is much contact with the outside world as monks or nuns come and go to work as teachers, nurses, social workers, etc. Many Roman Catholic convents are attached to a local church with members working alongside the priest in the community.

IN THE GLOSSARY

Abbot; Convent; Monastery; Monk; Mother Superior; Nun; Orthodox Church; Roman Catholic Church; Vocation.

WHAT DO YOU KNOW?

1 a What is the most important work that monks and nuns carry out?

b What is a 'vocation'?

c Who gave 'the Rule' by which monastic communities have lived ever since?

d Which three vows does a monk or a nun take when they enter their Religious Order?

e What is the difference between an 'open' and a 'closed' Religious Order?

2 What do you think has attracted many people over the centuries to live in a community dedicated to God?

3 What problems do you think there might be in a religious community if its members were not sworn to poverty, chastity and obedience?

2 People *and* events

THE SACRAMENTS

- **The sacraments are the most important services in most Christian Churches.**
- **In the Orthodox and Roman Catholic Churches there are seven sacraments but only two in the Protestant Churches.**
- **Many Christians believe that the sacraments bring a special blessing from God to those who receive them.**

The word 'sacrament' comes from the Latin word which means 'to make holy'. The sacraments are the most important services in most Christian churches. The Quakers and the Salvation Army, though, do not celebrate any of the sacraments. Protestant Churches, such as the Church of England and the Methodist Church, celebrate two of them whilst the Orthodox and Roman Catholic Churches celebrate seven. Each sacrament uses a symbol or symbols that people can touch and see, such as bread or wine, to bring a spiritual blessing.

A Jesus shared his last meal with his disciples. What is the link between this and the sacrament of Holy Communion?

1 The Protestant Church

Most Protestant Churches celebrate just the sacraments of the Eucharist (Holy Communion) and baptism. These are the only sacraments that can be traced directly back to the life and teaching of Jesus. Jesus was baptised by John the Baptist in the River Jordan and gave bread and wine to his disciples at a special meal so that they could remember him after he left the earth. Most Protestant churches believe that the value of these sacraments is that they help worshippers to remember Jesus.

2 The Orthodox and Roman Catholic Churches

Orthodox Christians and Roman Catholics along with some Anglicans believe that there are seven sacraments and that everyone who celebrates them receives a special spiritual blessing from God through doing so. The seven sacraments are:

a **Holy Communion**. This is the service at which Christians eat bread and drink wine together as they recall the last meal that Jesus ate with his disciples.

B Why is this person being anointed with oil?

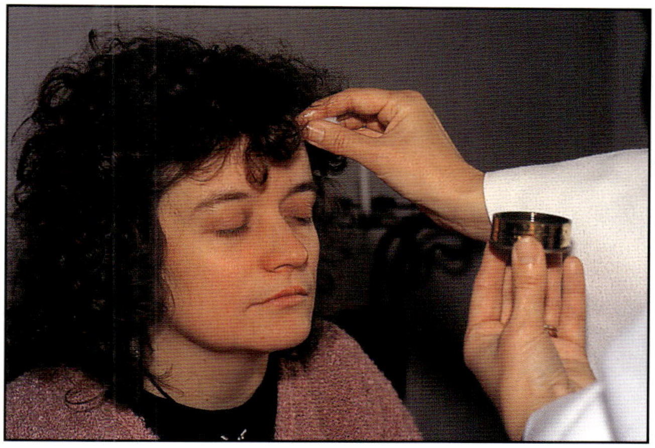

b **Baptism**. In most churches babies are baptised when water is poured over them although Baptists only baptise adults. In both cases the water shows the person's sins are forgiven by God.

c **Confirmation**. In confirmation a person 'confirms' the promises that others took for them when they were baptised as a baby. In the Orthodox Church chrismation is the equivalent of confirmation and takes place immediately after a baby is baptised. In other Churches, though, there is a gap between the two. After being baptised a person becomes a full member of the Church.

d **Reconciliation**. This is the sacrament of confession and forgiveness. A person confesses their sins to a priest and is assured that their sins have been forgiven by God.

e **Holy Orders**. This is the service of ordination at which men become priests.

f **Marriage**. In this sacrament a man and a woman promise that they will live together faithfully for the rest of their lives.

g **Anointing the sick**. In this sacrament someone who is very old, or ill, is anointed with oil as a sign of God's healing.

IN THE GLOSSARY

Anglican Church; Baptism; Chrismation; Confirmation; Eucharist; Holy Communion; Holy Orders; Ordination; Orthodox Church; Priest; Protestant; Quakers; Roman Catholic Church; Sacrament; Salvation Army.

WHAT DO YOU KNOW?

1 a What does the word 'sacrament' mean?

b Which two sacraments do most Protestant Churches celebrate?

c Why are these two sacraments of particular importance to Protestants?

d What are Christians reminded of when they take the sacrament of Holy Communion?

e What is the link between the sacraments of baptism and confirmation?

2 Roman Catholic and Anglican churches leave many years between baptism and confirmation whilst the Orthodox Church carries out the two sacraments in the same service. What do you think is the reasoning behind the two different approaches?

3 Why do the majority of Christians need the sacraments to help them understand, and worship, God?

HOLY COMMUNION

- **During the service of Holy Communion Christians celebrate the death and resurrection of Jesus.**
- **The symbols of bread and wine are used to help people remember the death of Jesus.**
- **The service of Holy Communion carries many different names and each one of them has its own special significance.**

The most important service in most churches is Holy Communion. This is the service during which Christians celebrate the death of Jesus for their sins and his rising from the dead (the resurrection). At this service worshippers come together to eat bread and drink wine just as Jesus did with his disciples at their last meal together.

A What are Christians remembering as they eat bread and drink wine together at Holy Communion?

Different names

Most Churches have their own name, and meaning, for this most important act of Christian worship:

a Roman Catholics call it the Mass. They believe that during the service the bread and wine become the body and blood of Jesus. This belief is called 'transubstantiation'.

b Orthodox Christians call it the Holy Liturgy. A 'liturgy' is a very old and largely unchanged service and the Holy Liturgy goes back to the fourth century.

c Anglicans call it the Eucharist (thanksgiving) or Holy Communion. Some Anglicans hold a similar view to Roman Catholics about the bread and wine whilst others are closer to the Nonconformists.

d Nonconformists call it the Breaking of Bread or the Lord's Supper. They believe that the Breaking of Bread is simply a time for remembering the death of Jesus and what it meant. The bread and wine help the people to do this.

In Holy Communion

In most Holy Communion services there are two parts

a The reading of the Bible, a short talk and prayers. In these prayers each worshipper seeks the forgiveness

B *In many churches the people come forward to the altar to receive the bread and wine.*

of God for their sins (the 'absolution') and remembers the needs of others ('intercessions'). In some services a Creed (a statement of belief) is recited by everyone together.

- The sharing of the bread and wine (see picture A). In many services worshippers give each other 'the kiss of peace' as it moves to a climax. The words of Jesus at the Last Supper are read as bread and wine are given to the worshippers (see picture B).

In Roman Catholic churches the Mass is celebrated each day as it is in some Anglican churches. In others, Holy Communion is usually celebrated each Sunday and once during the week. In many Anglican churches the main service on Sunday is now a Family Communion at which all ages celebrate communion. Those too young to have been confirmed are blessed by the priest as other members of the family take the bread and wine.

IN THE GLOSSARY

Absolution; Anglican Church; Bible; Breaking of Bread; Creed; Eucharist; Holy Communion; Holy Liturgy; Last Supper; Liturgy; Lord's Supper; Mass; Nonconformist Church; Orthodox Church; Priest; Quakers; Resurrection; Roman Catholic Church; Salvation Army; Transubstantiation.

WHAT DO YOU KNOW?

1 a **Which is the most important service in most churches?**

b **What do Roman Catholics believe happens during the Mass?**

c **What does the word 'Eucharist' mean?**

d **Which two names do Nonconformists use for their Holy Communion services?**

e **How do the different Churches differ in the way that they celebrate Holy Communion?**

2 **Why do Christians find the symbols of bread and wine helpful as they seek to remember the death and resurrection of Jesus?**

3 **Christians have disagreed amongst themselves about Holy Communion more than anything else over the centuries. Why do you think that this important service has led to so much disagreement?**

INFANT BAPTISM

- **Children join the Christian family through baptism.**
- **During the baptism service the priest makes the sign of the cross on the baby's forehead.**
- **The priest asks for the baby's forgiveness in the name of the Trinity – Father, Son and Holy Spirit.**

Many parents take their new baby to church to be baptised when it is a few months old. Infant baptism services are held in Anglican, Roman Catholic and Orthodox churches. There are three reasons why parents may want to have their baby baptised:

A *Where would you expect to find the font in a church? Why?*

a To thank God for its safe delivery. In the past this was very important as many babies, and mothers, died in childbirth or in the first few months following the birth. Even today there are many things that can go wrong around a birth although, thankfully, few now die as a result. Nevertheless, Christians believe that each baby is a gift from God and this is an opportunity to thank him for this.

b Baptism is the ceremony by which a young child is brought into membership of God's 'family' – the Church. The font, which holds the water for baptism, is traditionally placed just inside the door of a church since it is through baptism that the baby enters God's 'family'. Sometimes, though, the font is placed in the middle of the congregation so that the family of the church can give a warm welcome to the baby.

c Through baptism a baby receives God's forgiveness of sins as the water is poured over its head. The water symbolises the washing away of sin.

The service of infant baptism

For this service parents, godparents and the priest gather around the font. The priest asks the parents and godparents some questions about their own beliefs before going on to baptise the baby. He or she

B In which churches would you expect to see an infant baptism service?

then uses the water in the font to make the 'sign of the cross' on the baby's forehead before pouring it over the child's head three times 'in the Name of the Father, the Son and the Holy Spirit'. The water symbolises the cleansing of sin that the baby receives from God.

In Anglican and Methodist churches the parents of the baby are often handed a lighted candle during the service. They hold this as the priest tells the baby that the candle is a sign that he or she belongs to Christ who is the Light of the world. In the future the child is to let his or her light shine before everyone so that, seeing the child's good works, people may give their thanks to God in heaven for him or her. Baptist churches do not believe in infant baptism. Instead, they encourage members to bring their babies to church for a dedication service conducted by the minister. In this service the baby, and its future, are dedicated to the service of God.

IN THE GLOSSARY

Anglican Church; Baptism; Baptist Church; Font; Infant baptism; Methodist Church; Minister; Priest; Trinity.

WHAT DO YOU KNOW?

1 **a** Into which 'family' is a baby introduced through baptism?
   b Where is the water kept for infant baptism?
   c What does a baby receive as the water is poured over its head?
   d Why are the parents of the baby being baptised often handed a lighted candle during the service?
   e What is the difference between a service of infant baptism and a dedication service?

2 Why do you think confirmation (see pages 30 and 31) provides the opportunity for people to repeat the same promises which others made for them when they were baptised?

3 Many people criticise infant baptism because decisions and commitments are made by others on behalf of the baby. Do you think this is fair for people to do or should such commitments wait until a child is old enough to make his or her own decision?

2 People *and* events

CONFIRMATION

- **Confirmation is the time in some churches when people make the promises themselves that others made for them when they were baptised.**
- **At the confirmation service the bishop lays his hands on the head of each person.**
- **By the laying on of hands a person is given the strength of the Holy Spirit to lead a Christian life.**

For those who believe in infant baptism, confirmation is the time when people spiritually 'come of age'. The time at which this happens varies but in the Anglican and Roman Catholic Churches it is usually between the ages of 12 and 16. In the Orthodox Church, though, it is performed at the same time as baptism and called 'chrismation'. At confirmation those being confirmed make (confirm) for themselves the promises that were made by others at baptism.

A Where does the special authority of a bishop come from?

The confirmation service

Unlike infant baptism, confirmation is almost always conducted by a bishop. There is a good reason for this. When a person becomes a bishop he is always consecrated by three other bishops who, in turn, were consecrated by other bishops. This line of succession, it is believed, goes all the way back to the original apostles and, through them, to Jesus himself. This is where the special authority of the bishop originates.

After renewing their baptismal vows the bishop 'lays his hands' on the head of each person being confirmed. As he does so he prays: 'Confirm (make strong), O Lord, your servant with your Holy Spirit.' The strength and help of the Holy Spirit is given to the person being confirmed.

In the Roman Catholic confirmation service two interesting things take place:

B This shows one symbolic act performed during the confirmation service. Describe one other.

a The bishop makes the sign of the cross on the person's forehead with oil. Oil is a symbol of healing – in this case of inner, spiritual healing.

b The bishop lightly slaps the face of each person being confirmed with two fingers. This is a sign that all of the sins they have committed since they were baptised have been forgiven.

Why confirmation?

The service of confirmation is based on the 'laying on of hands' which is mentioned in the New Testament (Acts 8.14–17). The Church appears to have confirmed people since the fourth century CE. It has always been seen as a way of strengthening the faith of those who are new to Christianity. At a time when many of them were persecuted this was very important. It was also a way for people to show to the Christian community that they were serious in their wish to follow Jesus as a disciple.

IN THE GLOSSARY

Anglican Church; Apostle; Bishop; Chrismation; Confirmation; Infant baptism; New Testament; Orthodox Church; Roman Catholic Church.

WHAT DO YOU KNOW?

1 a Which priest usually conducts a confirmation service?

b What is meant by the 'laying on of hands'?

c What is a bishop giving to a person when he lays his hands on them?

d What is distinctive about a confirmation service in the Roman Catholic Church?

e What is the importance of a confirmation service – both to the Church and to the person being confirmed?

2 Why do you think people being confirmed are asked exactly the same questions asked of others when they were baptised? Why is it thought to be a good idea for them to revisit the questions?

3 What do you think is needed for a person to successfully live a Christian life? How might the service of confirmation help them to do this?

2 People *and* events

BELIEVER'S BAPTISM

- **Whilst most Churches baptise babies, the Baptist Church believes that only adult believers in Jesus should be baptised.**
- **Believer's baptism usually takes place in a pool at the front of the church.**
- **During believer's baptism the person is immersed fully beneath the water and this has important significance.**

Most Christian Churches baptise babies but the Baptist Church believes that only adult believers in Jesus should be baptised. Baptists dedicate babies to God but they do not offer baptism until someone is old enough to make their own commitment to Jesus Christ. In most Baptist churches there is a pool underneath the floorboards at the front (called a 'baptistry') for the service but some people prefer to be baptised in a local river or sea. Some Christians even travel to Israel to be baptised in the River Jordan and follow in the footsteps of Jesus.

A This banner makes three important points about baptism. What are they?

From the beginning of the Christian Church both men and women have worn white clothes for this ceremony – white being the symbol of purity and forgiveness. This practice is continued today with men wearing a white shirt and grey flannels and women wearing a white dress.

Believer's baptism

Nothing mysterious happens when a person is baptised. It is the symbolic meaning of the event that is important and not the event itself. This symbolism runs through the baptism itself during which:

a The person explains to everyone the reason why they want to be baptised. They have trusted in Jesus as their Saviour and now they wish to follow in his footsteps through the waters of baptism. As they go down a short flight of steps into the water they are showing that they are leaving their old, sinful life behind them. Their sins have been forgiven because they have put their trust in Jesus. Just as Jesus died

B At what age do you think a person is old enough to decide that they want to be baptised?

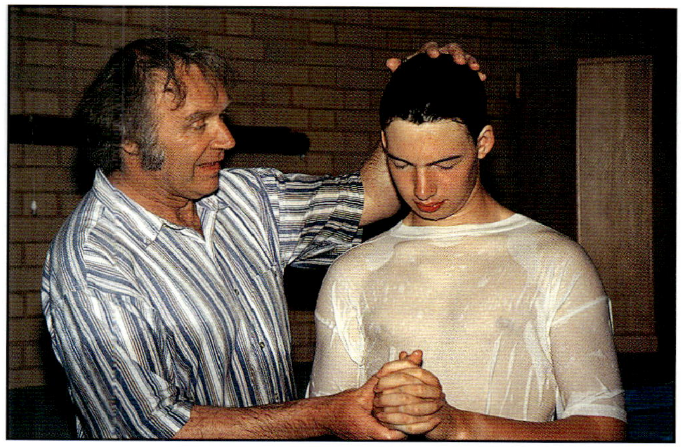

on the cross, they too are 'dying' in order to leave their old, sinful life behind.

b The minister rocks the person backwards until they are, for a few seconds, totally immersed in the water. This is why believer's baptism is often called 'baptism by immersion'. For the brief time that the person is beneath the water they are showing that they have died and are 'buried' with Christ. Just as Jesus was buried for two days in the unused tomb of Joseph of Arithmathea so the believer is buried with their Lord. This is the moment they leave their old, sinful life behind them for good.

c As they come up out of the water they leave the pool by a different set of steps to symbolise a new beginning. They have now entered into that new, resurrection life that they began to share with Jesus when they became a Christian. Jesus returned from the dead and entered into heaven to share God's eternal life. The baptised believer, too, enters into this eternal life which begins on earth and goes on forever in heaven.

IN THE GLOSSARY

Baptism; Baptist Church; Believer's baptism; Minister.

WHAT DO YOU KNOW?

1 **a** Which Church only baptises adult believers?

b What do Baptists mean when they speak of 'baptism by immersion'?

c What is happening symbolically as a person makes his or her way down the steps into the baptismal pool?

d Why are people said to be 'buried' with Christ when they are immersed beneath the water?

e Why do people who have just been baptised leave the pool by a different set of steps?

2 Speaking about faith in Christ (called 'giving a testimony') is a very important part of the whole adult baptismal experience. Why do you think people are expected to do this before they are baptised?

3 Imagine that you have just been baptised in a Baptist church. You feel that it is important to explain to your friends what has happened. How would you explain to them the importance of this step in your Christian life?

2 People *and* events

SEEKING FORGIVENESS

- **People come forward to the mercy seat in a Salvation Army citadel to seek God's forgiveness for their sins.**
- **Confessing sins to a priest is an important part of worship in many churches.**
- **Confession is now known as the 'Sacrament of Reconciliation' because the confession of sins is a step towards restoring a broken relationship with God.**

Being sorry for the wrong (sinful) things a person has done is a very important part of Christian worship. Christians believe in a holy God who can only accept worship from those who have been cleansed from their sins and forgiven. In some churches people confess their sins as they pray quietly to God with no one else being involved. This is what happens in most Protestant churches. These prayers are known as 'prayers of confession'. In other churches, though, people are given an opportunity to confess their sins in different ways. Here are two examples:

A *What obligation is this priest under as he listens to a person's confession?*

a The mercy seat

The mercy seat is a feature of all Salvation Army citadels. This is a platform at the front of the building where anyone can kneel to ask for God's forgiveness. Sometimes a service in the citadel ends with an invitation being given for anyone to come forward and kneel at the front. Sometimes someone else comes to kneel and pray with them. The mercy seat in the citadel is a symbol of God's love and forgiveness.

b The confessional

In Orthodox, Roman Catholic and some Anglican churches people regularly set aside time to confess their sins to a priest. Roman Catholics also go to confession at festivals and at other special times in the Christian year. The priest is not allowed to repeat to anyone else anything that he hears during a person's confession.

There are confessional boxes in some Roman Catholic churches (see picture A) but by no means all.

B *Do you think that people confessing their sins may be looking for more help than simply forgiveness?*

In modern Catholic churches confession is more likely to be heard by the priest sitting in a pew with the person (see picture B). In the older confessional box, though, there is a curtain or grill which separates the priest from the person. The priest is not supposed to know who is on the other side of the curtain although he will often, of course, recognise the person's voice.

Confession is now known within the Catholic Church as the Sacrament of Reconciliation. This is an important change. It recognises something which all Christians know to be true. Sinful actions separate them from God. Before they can worship him they must seek his forgiveness for their wrong actions. The priest, as God's representative, tells them that they can be forgiven if they confess their sins – and are truly sorry for what they have done. He may suggest to them that they perform a penance (penalty), such as saying some extra prayers, to show God how sorry they are. The priest may then place his hands on the person's head or shoulder and pray with them. He makes the 'sign of the cross' over them and gives them God's forgiveness – which is known as the 'absolution'.

IN THE GLOSSARY

Absolution; Anglican Church; Citadel; Mercy seat; Orthodox Church; Penance; Priest; Reconciliation; Roman Catholic Church; Salvation Army.

WHAT DO YOU KNOW?

1 a Why do Christians believe that someone must be forgiven for their sins before they can begin to worship God?

b What is the mercy seat and where would you expect to find one?

c How do priests in the Roman Catholic Church hear the confessions of those seeking God's forgiveness?

d Why is confession now called the Sacrament of Reconciliation in the Roman Catholic Church?

e What is the absolution?

2 It is sometimes said that 'confession is good for the soul'. What do you think this saying means?

3 If you wanted to find forgiveness for something you had done would you find it helpful to approach God through a priest, or would you want to pray to God alone for forgiveness?

2 People *and* events

MARRIAGE

- **People marry in a church to make their vows in the sight of God.**
- **Although human witnesses to marriage are required by law the most important witness to a church marriage is God.**
- **The vows which a couple make commit them to be faithful to each other until death separates them.**

There are some variations in the ways that different Churches celebrate marriage. For example, at a Roman Catholic wedding the couple give the vows, and the bread and wine of the Nuptual Mass, to each other. In some Orthodox weddings the couple walk around the church together to demonstrate that marriage has no beginning or end. They may also wear crowns in the second part of the service to show that they are the king and queen of their own kingdom – the house they will set up together.

A *If you were one of these two people marrying what would you hope for the future?*

The marriage service

People do not have to marry in church. Today couples can marry in any licensed building. Christian couples, though, feel that they want to make their vows to each other in the sight of God and enjoy God's blessing on their future married life. For most Christians being married in church is important. To make the wedding legal certain promises have to be made and at least two witnesses need to be present to sign the register along with the vicar. The most important witness at a Christian wedding, though, is God.

During the marriage service:

a The couple declare publicly that they know of no reason why they cannot be lawfully married. Obviously, if one or the other was already married that would make the marriage unlawful.

b The couple promise to love, comfort, honour, protect and be faithful to each other for as long as they both shall live. They then promise to look after one another from this moment onwards – for better and

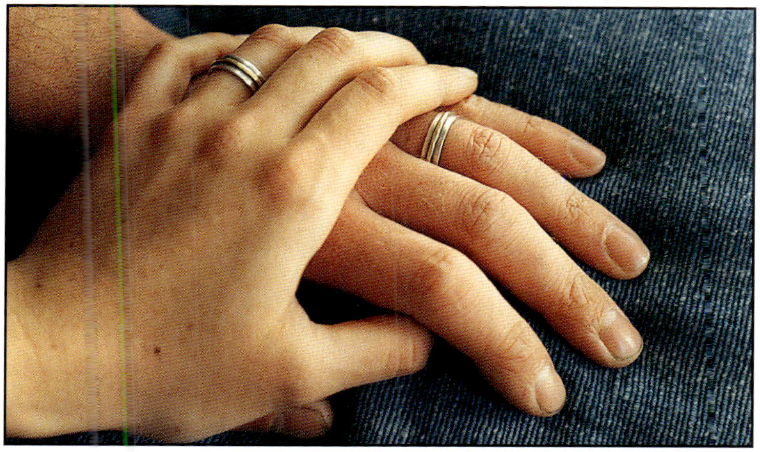

B Why do couples often exchange rings now during the wedding service?

worse, for richer and poorer, in sickness and in health, loving and cherishing one another. This is the solemn vow that they offer one another since this is what 'God's holy law' in the Bible demands.

c A ring is the symbol of a love that is endless and unbroken. Traditionally the groom has placed a ring on the finger of his bride but it is more common now for the couple to exchange rings with each other. The two rings then become visible symbols of their love for each other.

When the service has reached this stage the priest declares to everyone that the couple are now husband and wife 'in the name of the Father, the Son and the Holy Spirit.' He pronounces God's blessing on them and their life together. Then all the people at the wedding pray that God will help them in their future married life.

IN THE GLOSSARY

Bible; Mass; Orthodox Church; Priest; Roman Catholic Church; Sacrament.

WHAT DO YOU KNOW?

1 a What makes a Roman Catholic wedding distinctive?

b What is unusual about a wedding service in an Orthodox church?

c What makes a wedding legal in this country?

d What are the wedding vows?

e Who is the most important witness at a Christian wedding?

2 Some people today are calling for training to be given to those couples intending to marry. Do you think this is a good idea or not? If it is what do you think the training should cover?

3 Some churches will marry people who have been married before and have divorced. Other churches are strongly opposed to divorce. Do you think it is realistic to expect people now to promise to love someone 'until death us do part'?

2 People *and* events

DEATH

- **At the end of life the body disintegrates. Christians believe that the soul lives on.**
- **As death approaches a Roman Catholic is given a special Holy Communion, the viaticum, to provide them with spiritual food for the journey to come.**
- **The funeral service emphasises the Christian belief that life is eternal.**

Christians believe that each person is made up of two parts – the body and the soul or spirit. It is the physical part, the body, which disintegrates at death and returns to the earth before crumbling into dust. The spiritual part, the soul, survives death and lives for ever. Christians either bury the body after death or cremate (burn) it.

A *In which church are you most likely to see this coffin before a funeral service?*

The funeral service

Just as Christian beliefs about life after death differ, so do funeral services. As death approaches a Roman Catholic takes his or her last Holy Communion. This is called the 'viaticum' ('food for the journey'). The journey in question is the one that the soul takes after death. After death the body is sprinkled with holy water by the priest who is dressed in white robes. White is the colour usually associated in the Church with death and life after death. During the funeral service prayers are offered for the dead person.

The Orthodox Church does not recognise any difference between the living and the dead since they all belong to the one Church. The body is washed, dressed in new clothes and laid in an open coffin. This allows everyone to say goodbye to the dead person until the moment they are buried. A strip of cloth is laid across the corpse's forehead and an icon placed in its hand. The body is covered by a cloth to show that everyone who has died is under the protection of Jesus.

A funeral service in every church will contain prayers entrusting the care of the dead person to God. The service also frequently underlines the Christian belief that death is not the end – life is eternal. This means that death is not only a time of great sadness

B What message can you see on this gravestone about life after death?

but also a time of looking forward with hope and joy. After death a gravestone can be erected over the grave (see picture B) or the ashes of someone cremated can be scattered in a place of some personal significance.

Life after death

Christians believe strongly in life after death. It is not easy, though, to imagine just what that life will be like. They take their teaching on the matter from the Bible and this reinforces the belief that Christians will spend eternity in the presence of God. Before this happens, however, there is a time of judgement to be faced. In the Bible this appears to be a straightforward matter of dividing the good, bound for heaven, from the evil, bound for hell. However, many Christians find this teaching difficult to accept. Roman Catholics believe that almost everyone spends time in 'purgatory' being 'prepared' for heaven since no one can enter straight into the presence of God.

IN THE GLOSSARY

Bible; Holy Communion; Icon; Orthodox Church; Priest; Purgatory; Roman Catholic Church; Viaticum.

WHAT DO YOU KNOW?

1 a What part of the human personality do Christians believe survives death?

b What is the 'viaticum'?

c What is different about a funeral service held in an Orthodox church and one held in any other church?

d What do Christians believe about life after death?

e What is purgatory?

2 The Christian belief about life after death depends on accepting that there is a spiritual as well as a physical part of every human being. Do you agree with this and, if so, what leads you to believe it?

3 Do you think that believing in a life after death should affect the way that people live their lives in this life? If so, in what ways would you expect this to be the case?

2 People *and* events

SYMBOLS

- **Symbols are very important in Christian worship.**
- **Symbols help people to understand abstract, spiritual realities.**
- **Different colours and clothes used in Christian worship carry important spiritual messages.**

Christian churches and places of worship are full of symbols. Symbols are a very important part of Christian worship. Often symbols are the only way of explaining the spiritual aspects of this worship. This was particularly true when the majority of churches were built and most people were badly educated or illiterate. They needed 'pictures' to help them worship. They were surrounded by them every time they came to church.

The use of colour in church

Colours are often used in church as symbols. Many Anglican and Roman Catholic churches cover their altars, and other symbols, on Good Friday (see pages 56–7) with black or purple cloths. This is the day on which people come to church to spend time remembering the death of Jesus on the cross. Two days later, on Easter Day (see pages 58–9), the mood changes as Christians celebrate the resurrection of Jesus from the dead and the dark colours of Good Friday are replaced by whites and yellows suggesting new life. Spring flowers are used as symbols of new life and birth.

Seven weeks after Easter the Church celebrates the last major festival of the Christian Year. This is the festival of Pentecost (Whitsun) at which the Church remembers the giving of the Holy Spirit to the early Christians (see pages 60–1). The writer of the Acts of the Apostles, Luke, described the event in which he wrote of 'tongues of fire' coming down from heaven and settling on each of the disciples. Red is the dominant colour in church at this time.

A *Statues of St Peter always show him with a set of keys. Why?*

B Some churches have candles on their altars. Can you find out what candles in a church symbolise?

Clothes

Symbolic clothes play an important part in the life and worship of the Church. The clothes worn by bishops, priests and ministers all contain many symbolic elements. Most of them wear a dog-collar around their neck which reminds everyone of the halter worn around the necks of slaves to prevent them from escaping. It is a reminder to everyone who serves in the church and community that each of them is 'enslaved' to God.

The traditional habit worn by many nuns is highly symbolic. Everyone dressed the same indicates that all people are equal and that no one is more important than anyone else. The veil and the long dress are symbols of modesty and humility. The plain black colour shows that the person has no material possessions of her own – she has taken the vow of poverty. The belt around the waist is tied with three knots as a reminder that each nun takes a three fold vow. Along with poverty each nun promises to live a life of chastity (no sexual relations) and obedience.

IN THE GLOSSARY

Altar; Anglican Church; Bishop; Easter Day; Good Friday; Minister; Nun; Pentecost; Priest; Roman Catholic Church; Whitsun.

WHAT DO YOU KNOW?

1 a What do Anglicans and Roman Catholics do on Good Friday to emphasise the holiness and seriousness of the day?

b What do Christians celebrate on Easter Day?

c How do the dominant colours in church change between Good Friday and Easter Day?

d Which colour predominates in church on Whitsun? Why?

e Why do priests wear 'dog-collars'?

2 Someone has said that many churches use different colours at different times of the year to create the appropriate mood for the season. How do colours help to create the right mood?

3 Do you think we still need symbols today? Describe two symbols used in everyday life which illustrate aspects of life that would otherwise be difficult to understand.

2 People *and* events

MUSIC

- **The singing of psalms in Christian worship is a tradition going back to the Old Testament.**
- **Thousands of hymns have been written for use in Christian worship.**
- **Worship in church is sometimes led by a choir and the singing is usually accompanied by an organ.**

In the Old Testament people sang and played musical instruments as they prayed to God. Many of these old songs – psalms – are included in the Bible in the book of Psalms. Music has played a very important part in Church worship for centuries and it still does. Music was clearly important in the early Christian church as Paul encouraged Christians of the time to 'Sing psalms, hymns and sacred songs; sing to God with thanksgiving in your hearts.' (Colossians 3.16)

Hymns – old and new

Anglican and Roman Catholic churches still sing the old psalms as part of their worship in some of their services. Hymns rather than psalms, though, have proved to be much more popular in Christian worship. More than one million hymns have been written in the English language alone. Some of them, such as 'Abide with me' and 'Rock of Ages', have become favourites, even with people who do not go to church. Perhaps the most popular hymn-writer of all time was Charles Wesley who wrote over 1,000 hymns in the eighteenth century. Many of Wesley's hymns are still used regularly in Christian worship today. Charles Wesley was the brother of John, the founder of the Methodist Church, and his hymns are particularly popular in this Church. As most of the people in the past could not read or write the hymns were learned off by heart. They became very valuable ways of teaching people different aspects of Christian belief.

Chants and modern songs

Many of the chants used today in Christian worship go back to the seventh or eighth century. These are

A *The Orthodox Church does not allow singing to be accompanied. Why?*

***B** Why are choirs often only found today in large churches and cathedrals?*

Gregorian chants that have been kept alive over the centuries by monks and nuns singing them in their monasteries and convents. Chants which come from the modern monastic community of Taize, in southern France, are even more popular today, especially amongst young people. Thousands of people, young and old, spend some time in the community each year and take its music back to their own churches.

It is an old tradition that music in church was led by an organ and a choir. Some churches still have their own choirs but the best choirs are now usually found leading worship in the cathedrals. Many years ago these choirs were all-male. Girls and women were later allowed to become members as male recruitment became more difficult. Often smaller churches now use music groups to lead their worship. Modern hymns and songs have been written in recent years for these groups to play. This new music is particularly popular in the worship of Nonconformist churches and House Churches.

IN THE GLOSSARY

Anglican Church; Bible; Cathedral; House Church; Hymn; Methodist Church; Monk; Nonconformist Church; Nun; Old Testament; Psalm; Roman Catholic Church.

WHAT DO YOU KNOW?

1 a What are the songs called which played a part in worship in the Old Testament?
b Who encouraged Christians to sing psalms, hymns and sacred songs?
c Who wrote more than 1,000 hymns?
d Why were hymns so valuable in the past?
e How were Gregorian chants kept alive over the centuries?

2 Why do you think that singing plays such an important part in Christian worship? What might worshippers gain from singing together?

3 The Salvation Army founder, William Booth, asked the question: 'Why should the Devil have all the best tunes?' What point do you think he was making? Find out what is distinctive about the music used in worship in a Salvation Army citadel.

3 Celebrations

THE CHRISTIAN YEAR

- **The Christian Year begins with Advent and the Christmas cycle.**
- **The most important time of the year for all Christians begins with Lent and goes through to Good Friday and Easter Day.**
- **The final major festival of the Christian Year is Pentecost at which Christians remember the giving of the Holy Spirit to the Church.**

The Church festivals are scattered throughout the year and remind worshippers of the main events in the life of Jesus and the early Church. The Christian Year begins with the festivals of Advent, Christmas and Epiphany. The period from Advent through to Epiphany is known as the 'Christmas Cycle'. The 'Easter Cycle' begins with Lent and ends, seven weeks later, with Easter Day. The final cycle, Whitsun, is the least important of the three and contains several festivals although only one, Whitsun, is celebrated by all Christians.

The Christmas Cycle

Advent is a time of preparation for the coming festival of Christmas. During the four weeks of Advent Christians prepare their hearts and minds for the coming of Jesus to the stable in Bethlehem. This coming is a miracle to Christians because Jesus, the Son of God, was born as a human being – an event known as the 'Incarnation'. The five candles on the Advent wreath are lit on the four Sundays and on Christmas morning to represent the coming of Jesus, the Light of the world. During Advent Christians also think about the Second Coming of Jesus into the world at the end of time.

The Easter Cycle

A gap of several weeks separates Christmas from the time of preparation for the most important Christian festival – Easter. This time of preparation, Lent, begins with Ash Wednesday when, traditionally, people receive an ash cross marked on their forehead by the priest. Ash is the Biblical symbol of repentance and forgiveness and this is what Lent is all about. It follows

A *This shows a Christingle service. Do you know which festival this is linked with?*

B This shows a Good Friday procession. What are Christians celebrating on this day?

the example of Jesus who spent 40 days in the desert fasting before being tempted by the Devil. During Lent many Christians spend more time than usual praying, reading their Bible and meeting with other believers to study their faith.

Lent ends with Holy Week when Christians remember the events in the last week of the life of Jesus. This begins with Palm Sunday on which Jesus entered the city of Jerusalem on a donkey. On Maundy Thursday they return to the last meal that Jesus ate with his disciples. On Good Friday they spend time in church remembering the death of Jesus on the cross whilst on Easter Day they celebrate the resurrection of Jesus from the dead.

IN THE GLOSSARY

Advent; Ash Wednesday; Bible; Christmas; Devil; Easter Day; Epiphany; Fasting; Good Friday; Holy Spirit; Holy Week; Incarnation; Lent; Maundy Thursday; Palm Sunday; Pentecost; Second Coming; Whitsun.

The Pentecost cycle

The last cycle of the Christian Year takes place at Pentecost (Whitsun) when Christians celebrate the event that led to the birth of the Christian Church – the giving of the Holy Spirit to the early Christians in Jerusalem.

WHAT DO YOU KNOW?

1 a When does the Christian Year begin?

b What is the relationship between Advent and Christmas?

c What event is known to Christians as the 'Incarnation'?

d Why do many Christians have an ash cross placed on their forehead at the beginning of Lent?

e What happens during Holy Week?

2 During Advent and Lent people spend more time in prayer and Bible study than at other times of the year. What part do you think this might play in preparing them for the festivals of Christmas and Easter?

3 Christians disagree over the value of different festivals. What arguments do you think can be put forward for holding festivals to celebrate the most important events in the life of Jesus and the early Church?

3 Celebrations

ADVENT

- **The season of Advent marks the beginning of the Christian Year for many churches.**
- **At Advent Christians remember the coming of John the Baptist and Jesus and the future return of Jesus to the earth.**
- **Advent candles and wreaths are an important part of the festival.**

The Christian Year begins with Advent at the end of November or the beginning of December. There are four Sundays in Advent altogether leading up to the celebration of the birth of Jesus on Christmas Day.

Looking back and forward

The word Advent means 'coming' and this introduces the theme for the weeks leading up to Christmas in many churches. The Anglican and Roman Catholic Churches keep this time as a preparation for the birth of Jesus. The festival has two emphases:

a A time for looking back. The Bible readings, prayers, hymns and sermons during Advent look back first to the coming of John the Baptist into the world. John was the cousin of Jesus who, according to the Gospels, was sent by God to prepare the people for the coming of Jesus. Advent also recalls the 'coming' of Jesus to be born in a stable in Bethlehem.

b A time for looking forward. As Christians celebrate Advent they look forward to the Second Coming of Jesus into the world. Since the birth of the Christian Church it has been the belief of Christians that Jesus would return to judge and then rule over the world.

A Find out the significance of this Advent candle.

Celebrating Advent

Nonconformist churches do not celebrate Advent. In those churches that do, however, the first Sunday in Advent is marked by a procession carrying a lighted candle into a darkened church. As we shall see, candles play a very important role in Advent celebrations. They are a reminder to everyone that the coming of Jesus brought light (the light of God) into a dark world. One of the most memorable descriptions by Jesus of himself was to call himself 'the Light of the world'.

B Why are there five candles on this Advent wreath?

During Advent readings from the Bible play a very important role in church services. The readings chosen emphasise:

a The creation of the world – the descriptions from the early chapters of the Bible in the book of Genesis.

b Psalms from the Old Testament.

c The passages from the Old Testament which speak of Jesus as God's chosen Messiah – the leader that the Jewish people were waiting for.

d The story of John the Baptist who prepared the people for the coming of Jesus.

The decorations in church during Advent suit the mood of the season. Many churches are decked out in mauve or purple. Advent candles are lit (see picture A). An Advent crown or wreath (see picture B) at the front of the church contains five candles with a new one being lit on each of the four Sundays of Advent. The fifth candle is lit on Christmas Day itself. This means that the amount of light coming from the wreath builds up as Christmas itself approaches.

IN THE GLOSSARY

Advent; Anglican Church; Bible; Christmas; Gospel; Messiah; Nonconformist Church; Old Testament; Psalm; Roman Catholic Church; Second Coming; Sermon; Sunday.

WHAT DO YOU KNOW?

1 a How many Sundays are there in Advent?
b What does the word 'Advent' mean?
c Which three events are remembered at Advent?
d How do candles play a very important part in the season of Advent?
e Why are candles a very important symbol associated with Advent?

2 Why do you think that light is seen as being an important symbol to explain the meaning of the Advent season?

3 As they enter church on the first Sunday of Advent each person is given a lighted candle so that the building is gradually bathed in light. What do you think the people are intended to understand by this?

3 Celebrations

CHRISTMAS

- **Christmas is the festival in which Christians celebrate the birth of Jesus.**
- **Midnight Mass marks the beginning of Christmas Day in many churches.**
- **Epiphany celebrates the visit of the Wise Men to see the infant Jesus.**

Christmas is the most popular Christian festival and is celebrated throughout the world on 25 December. This is the day on which Christians remember the birth of Jesus in a stable in Bethlehem. However, no one knows when Jesus was born. Orthodox Christians believe that the old, traditional date for the birth, 6 January, is the most suitable time to celebrate it. Most Churches though celebrate the event on 25 December and have done so since the fourth century when Christians took over a festival day dedicated in the Roman Empire to the worship of the sun. They celebrate the festival of Epiphany on 6 January.

A The crib is a visual symbol. What do you think Christians might learn from a scene like this in church?

Midnight Mass, celebrated on Christmas Eve and spilling over into Christmas Day, is the best attended service of the year in most churches. Worship at this service, with carols and Bible readings, concentrates on the accounts in Matthew's and Luke's Gospels of the birth of Jesus. There is a crib in most churches showing Mary, Joseph, the baby Jesus and animals. The figures are often placed in the crib by children before Christmas with the baby being added on Christmas morning. In many churches the dark colours of Advent are now replaced by the white and gold of Christmas symbolising the purity and kingship of Jesus.

Christmas is a very traditional time for most families. However, many of the traditions linked with it carry little religious significance. For example, the Christmas tree and Christmas cards go back no further than Victorian times.

Epiphany

Although it is not a major festival many churches mark the feast of Epiphany 12 days after Christmas Day. This festival, one of the most important celebrated by the early Christians, originally remembered the baptism of Jesus by John the Baptist in the River Jordan. Now, though, it is linked with the visit of the Wise Men to see the infant Jesus. The Gospel story tells how they

B Shepherds and the Wise Men visited the infant Jesus. What do you think people were meant to learn from this?

were guided by a special star to the stable in which Jesus lay. Their visit to Jesus has always been considered important because these three astrologers were the first non-Jews (Gentiles) to see the infant Jesus. This emphasised the belief of the early Christians that Jesus was the Saviour of everyone – Jews and non-Jews alike.

The Gospels also tell us that the Wise Men brought three gifts to Jesus and that each of them had symbolic significance in Jesus' later life:

a Gold – to show that he was a king.

b Frankincense – to indicate that he was a priest who would bring people back to God. Burning frankincense smells sweet and so was used in the worship of God.

c Myrrh – to show that he had come into the world to suffer and die. Myrrh was used to embalm dead bodies.

IN THE GLOSSARY

Advent; Bible; Christmas; Crib; Epiphany; Gospel; Orthodox Church; Priest; Virgin Mary.

WHAT DO YOU KNOW?

1 a **On which two dates do different Christians celebrate the birth of Jesus?**

b **What is Midnight Mass?**

c **Which two colours are used in many churches to symbolise Christmas? What do these colours symbolise?**

d **What is celebrated by many churches on Epiphany?**

e **What was the symbolic importance of the three gifts brought by the Wise Men to the infant Jesus?**

2 **Not every Christian believes that Wise Men visited Jesus but most of them think that the story has something important to say about Jesus. What do you think this is?**

3 **For over three centuries Christians did not celebrate the birth of Jesus. They did not know when Jesus was born. Then they took over a pagan festival to celebrate the event. Does that strike you as odd? Why?**

3 Celebrations

LENT

- **Easter is the most important festival in the Christian Year.**
- **The season of Lent is a time of prayer and preparation leading up to Easter.**
- **Lent begins with Ash Wednesday, the day on which an ash cross is smeared on the forehead of each worshipper.**

Christmas may be the most popular Christian festival but Easter is the most important. This is the time when Christians remember the death of Jesus (Good Friday) and his resurrection from the dead (Easter Day). As with Christmas, though, there is a time of preparation for Easter before the festival begins. This time is called 'Lent'. During this time Christians try to spend more time than usual praying and reading their Bible. They know that the death and resurrection of Jesus are the two most important events in their faith.

A *Why do you think Jesus was tempted in the desert by Satan?*

The temptations of Jesus

Lent lasts for 40 days and runs through to Easter Saturday. It corresponds with the 40 days that Jesus spent in the wilderness (desert) of Judea before his life's ministry began. Jesus had just been baptised and this was followed by a time of fasting (going without food) and temptation at the hands of Satan, the Devil. During this time Satan tried to persuade Jesus to follow an easier path seeking popularity with the people rather than doing God's will. Taking their lead from the experience of Jesus at the hands of Satan many Christians over the centuries have used Lent as a time for fasting and penitence. Today, however, the fasting has long since disappeared at Lent. Some people, though, still try some act of self-denial to show how serious they are about following the Christian way of life.

Shrove Tuesday and Ash Wednesday

Shrove Tuesday is the day before Lent begins. This was the day on which people used to make pancakes to use up all the fat in the house before the serious

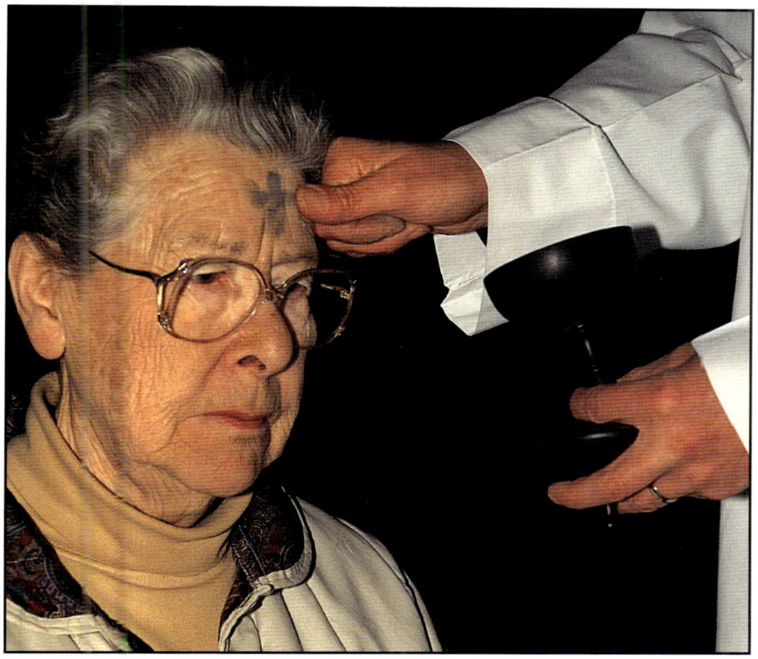

B *Where does the ash used on Ash Wednesday come from?*

On the following day, Ash Wednesday, the priests in some churches draw an ash cross on the forehead of each worshipper during a service of Holy Communion. Ash is the traditional symbol of repentance and sorrow for sin going back to the Old Testament. Christians are accepting that it was their sins, and those of the whole human race, that caused the death of Jesus on the cross. The ash that the priest uses comes from the burning of the palm crosses given out in church on the previous Palm Sunday.

fasting of Lent began. They also went to church on this day to be 'shriven' (forgiven) by the priest. Having confessed their sins each person was given a penance to perform to show that they were truly sorry for what they had done. The idea of being forgiven for one's sins is at the heart of Lent. Shrove Tuesday has long since lost any real religious significance but is still celebrated as 'Pancake Day'.

IN THE GLOSSARY

Ash Wednesday; Bible; Christmas; Easter; Fasting; Good Friday; Holy Communion; Lent; Old Testament; Palm Sunday; Priest; Satan; Shrove Tuesday.

WHAT DO YOU KNOW?

1 a What do Christians remember on Good Friday and Easter Day?
b What is Lent?
c Which event in the life of Jesus is the background to the season of Lent?
d Why is Shrove Tuesday so-called?
e What happens on Ash Wednesday?

2 As the priest marks ash on a person's forehead he or she tells them: 'Remember, O man, that dust thou art and to dust thou shalt return.' Why do you think each worshipper is reminded of this on Ash Wednesday?

3 The season of Lent is concerned with sin, repentance and forgiveness. Some people think that any talk of sin is very old-fashioned and out-of-date today. Do you think that the word 'sin' still has meaning for people today. If so, what do you think sin is?

3 Celebrations

PALM SUNDAY

- **Palm Sunday is the first day of Holy Week.**
- **On Palm Sunday Christians remember the time that Jesus rode into the city of Jerusalem on the back of a donkey.**
- **Many churches recreate the entry of Jesus into Jerusalem by leading a procession behind a donkey.**

Christians remember the events that took place in the last week of the life of Jesus during Holy Week. This very important week in the life of the Church begins with Palm Sunday and goes through Maundy Thursday to Good Friday. Palm Sunday celebrates the first time that Jesus entered the holy city of Jerusalem with his disciples. The event is remembered, in particular, because of the unusual way that Jesus approached the city which stood at the heart of the Jewish faith.

A Why are these people taking part in a procession on Palm Sunday?

The Passover

By the time of Jesus Jewish people had been scattered through the whole of the Roman Empire. Those who did not live in Israel tried to keep their faith alive even though thousands of them were not within reach of a synagogue. One of the ways in which they did this was to keep the different festivals. There were three 'Pilgrimage' festivals which Jewish people tried to celebrate in the city of Jerusalem. One of these Pilgrimage festivals was the Passover or Pesach.

The Passover was the most important Jewish festival. It was very important because of the event that it commemorated. Centuries earlier the Jews had spent more than 400 years as slaves in Egypt but God had finally sent them a deliverer. His name was Moses and through a series of miracles the Jews escaped from Egypt under his leadership. This was the event, the most important in Jewish history, that Jews celebrated each year during the Passover festival. It was this that brought Jesus, and his disciples, to Jerusalem.

Entering Jerusalem

Whilst thousands of Jewish pilgrims arrived in Jerusalem for the Passover on foot Jesus arrived in a different way – on the back of a donkey. His followers believed that he was fulfilling prophecies in the Old

B *Does it surprise you that the mood of the people welcoming Jesus here could change within a few days to one demanding his death?*

Testament by arriving in this way. The people believed that God had sent them their long-promised leader, the Messiah. They laid out their coats and threw palm leaves on the road in front of him. This was the kind of welcome normally reserved for a king.

Christians believe that this was a very important event in the life of Jesus. It took place at the start of the week which was to end with his death. The same people who welcomed Jesus as their Messiah turned against him and demanded his death a few days later. To enter into the spirit of this day as much as possible Christians meet together in church, collect small palm crosses and then form a procession outside the building. Often they are led by a donkey carrying a small child on its back. As the people follow behind they sing hymns which are associated with the last few days in the life of Jesus. They are demonstrating their faith in Jesus to the people who do not go to church and offering Jesus to them as their Saviour and Lord.

IN THE GLOSSARY

Good Friday; Holy Week; Hymn; Jerusalem; Maundy Thursday; Messiah; Old Testament; Passover.

WHAT DO YOU KNOW?

1 a When do Christians remember the events that took place in the last week of Jesus' life?

b What do Christians remember on Palm Sunday?

c What was unusual about the way Jesus entered Jerusalem during the Passover festival?

d What do Jews commemorate during the Passover festival?

e How do Christians often celebrate Palm Sunday?

2 Imagine that you live in a house which overlooks a Palm Sunday procession. How would you describe what you have seen and its meaning to a friend?

3 What do you think an outsider might make of a Palm Sunday procession? Do you think this is an effective way of communicating the Christian message or not?

3 Celebrations

MAUNDY THURSDAY

- **Maundy Thursday takes its name from the new commandment that Jesus gave to his disciples – to love one another.**
- **At the Last Supper Jesus washed the feet of his disciples to show them that his followers must be humble.**
- **Using a loaf of bread and a cup of wine Jesus gave his disciples a meal by which to remember him.**

The day on which Christians remember Jesus eating his last meal with his disciples is called Maundy Thursday. The word 'Maundy' comes from the Latin word 'mandatum' meaning 'commandment'. It was during this last meal (the Last Supper) that Jesus told his disciples that he was giving them a new commandment – that they should love one another. They were familiar, as Jews, with the Ten Commandments from the Jewish Scriptures but here was another one – a special one from Jesus.

A *Do you think it is surprising that Jesus should take an oridinary act (breaking bread) to convey the most important spiritual truths to his disciples?*

Washing feet

Just one of the Gospels tells us that Jesus acted out a parable in front of his disciples to teach them what it meant to be a disciple. They knew that a person's feet were hot and dusty after travelling and it was the custom for the lowest servant in the house to bring water and a towel to wash them.

Jesus took them completely by surprise when he did just that for his disciples. He tied a towel around his waist and washed their feet. They were amazed and one of them, Peter, objected. Jesus, though, wanted to teach them that all of his followers were called by God to serve others. In some Roman Catholic churches the priest washes the feet of 12 members of his congregation following the example of Jesus.

B Why do you think Nonconformists call Holy Communion the Breaking of Bread?

A new feast

Maundy Thursday is even more important because on this day Jesus gave the Church its most precious act of worship. As Jesus ate his last meal with his disciples he told them about his coming death in Jerusalem. He had tried to do this before but they failed to understand. Now he used two common objects as symbols:

a A loaf of bread. Jesus broke the loaf into many pieces and gave a piece to each of his disciples. The bread, he explained to them, was just like his body which was shortly to be broken into many pieces.

b A goblet of wine. In the old Jewish sacrifices the blood of an animal was smeared on the altar and because of this God forgave the sins of the people. Shortly his own blood was going to be spilt and, through it, everyone's sins could be forgiven.

Bread and wine are at the heart of the service of Holy Communion. Christians come together on Maundy Thursday to remember that within hours of giving these two symbols to his disciples Jesus died on a cross. Together they celebrate Holy Communion – the most serious celebration of this service in the Christian year.

IN THE GLOSSARY

Gospel; Holy Communion; Maundy Thursday; Peter; Priest; Roman Catholic Church; Ten Commandments.

WHAT DO YOU KNOW?

1 a What does the word 'Maundy' mean and why is it associated with this day?

b What did Jesus hope to teach his disciples by washing their feet?

c Which act of worship in the church has its origins on the first Maundy Thursday?

d What did Jesus want his followers to learn from the loaf of bread he broke in front of them?

e What did Jesus want his followers to learn from the goblet of wine he shared with them?

2 Jesus acted out more than one parable in his ministry to teach his followers important spiritual truths. Why do you think Jesus found this useful?

3 Often Jesus tried to share with his disciples the news that he was shortly going to die. Each time they failed to understand what he was saying to them. Why do you think they found this so difficult to grasp?

3 Celebrations

GOOD FRIDAY

- **Good Friday is the most serious day in the whole Christian Year.**
- **On Good Friday Christians remember the death of Jesus on the cross**
- **The most important service on Good Friday in many churches is a vigil when Christians watch with Jesus in his last few hours.**

The Friday of Holy Week, called Good Friday, is the most serious day in the whole Christian Year. To underline this all moveable furnishings are taken out of Anglican and Roman Catholic churches whilst the others are covered by dark cloths. There are no flowers or candles visible in church. Often, though, a simple wooden cross is left standing in a central place (see picture A). The starkness of the place of worship represents the loneliness of Jesus on the cross dying abandoned by everyone. For a time Jesus even thought that God, his Father, had abandoned him.

A What does the position of this cross above the altar tell you about the importance of the death of Jesus to Christians?

In some places churches of different denominations come together on Good Friday for a march of witness. Even though they disagree about many things Christians from different Churches are united in their response to the death of Jesus. They march behind someone carrying a large wooden cross to a central place where they hold a service. They try to explain to people around them the importance of the death of Jesus to everyone.

Celebrating Good Friday

Some churches encourage worshippers to share a little of the loneliness of Jesus on the cross. They hold a 'vigil', a time of watching with Jesus, for the last three hours that Jesus spent on the cross (see picture B). As far as we know that was between the hours of 12 noon and 3pm. During this time the church is open for people to sit quietly and meditate on the last words that Jesus spoke before his death. The Gospels tell us that Jesus spoke seven times from the cross and these words have been highly treasured by Christian believers ever since.

In Orthodox churches believers hold a kind of funeral for Jesus on Good Friday. A cloth bearing an image of the dead Christ is carried into the centre of the church

B *The cross is the most important Christian symbol. What does it symbolise?*

in front of the people. The worshippers then follow the cloth as it is carried in a procession around the outside of the buildings while the church bells ring. Finally the cloth is brought back into the middle of the church to remind worshippers of the burial of Jesus in the tomb belonging to Joseph of Arithmathea. This links up with the way that Orthodox worshippers greet the first few minutes of Easter morning.

Why 'Good' Friday?

On the surface it would seem strange to call the day on which a cruel death is remembered 'Good'. The day, though, has always been called Good Friday because of the goodness of Jesus. Christians believe that Jesus came into the world so that he could die. They believe that the death of Jesus opened up the way to God for everyone who believes in Jesus. Everyone's sins can now be forgiven and each person offered a new start, the beginning of eternal life. That is what makes this day 'good' for Christian believers.

IN THE GLOSSARY

Anglican Church; Easter; Good Friday; Gospel; Holy Week; Orthodox Church; Roman Catholic Church; Vigil.

WHAT DO YOU KNOW?

1 a What is a vigil?

b How many hours do some Christians spend in church on Good Friday? What are they doing?

c What do believers hold in an Orthodox church to remember the death of Jesus?

d Why do some churches hold a march of witness on Good Friday? What is the march intended to demonstrate?

e Why is this day called 'Good' Friday?

2 What do you think people might gain by spending time in church and 'watching' with Jesus through the last hours of his life?

3 Why do many churches choose Good Friday as the day on which to demonstrate to others that they are united in important matters?

3 Celebrations

EASTER DAY

- **Easter Day is the most important day in the Christian Year.**
- **Christians celebrate the resurrection of Jesus from the dead on Easter Day.**
- **Easter commemorates the birth of new life, the bringing of light into great darkness.**

Easter Day is the most important day of the year for all Christians. It is the day on which they celebrate the rising of Jesus from the dead – an event known to Christians as 'the resurrection'. Paul believed that if Jesus had not risen from the dead then the whole Christian faith would have been a waste of time.

A *Why is it very important for Christians to believe that Jesus rose from the dead?*

Celebrating Easter

The date of the Christmas festival is the same each year but that of Easter is 'moveable'. The date of Easter is fixed each year by the position of the moon. In practice this means that it can occur at any time between 21 March and 24 April. In many Anglican, Roman Catholic and Orthodox churches the first celebration of Easter begins late on the Saturday evening. The service, called a 'vigil', begins with the church in total darkness although one or two candles illuminate a Bible from which readings are taken. The overall darkness of the church shows that Jesus is still dead in the tomb. Everyone in the congregation is holding a candle although none of them are yet lit. After the readings the priest lights a fire at the back of the church and from this he lights the Paschal Candle. The Candle is carried to the front of the church with the priest stopping three times to say 'The light of Christ' to which the people reply 'Thanks be to God'. Jesus referred to himself in John's Gospel as the 'Light of the World'.

Each time this happens a few more candles are lit and these pass the flame on to others. The light spreads through the church as the doors are swung open and the priest announces in a loud voice 'The Lord is risen' with the people replying 'He is risen indeed'. The people turn to each other and greet one another with a holy kiss. Church bells are rung for the first time in three days and the people take Holy

B This cross covered with flowers is saying something very important about Easter. What is it?

Communion. Whilst the Eucharistic meal on Maundy Thursday was serious and solemn the one on Easter Day is joyful and hopeful.

Easter traditions

There are many traditions associated with this day and all of them are connected with the Easter theme of new life. Christians believe not just that Jesus rose from the dead in Palestine but that he is alive in today's world. All those who believe in him can share in his resurrection life. This eternal life begins here and now but stretches forward to eternity.

Easter gardens are an important feature in many churches. These gardens contain an empty tomb and three empty crosses standing in a garden containing herbs and flowers. Easter eggs symbolise the new life which is at the heart of Easter Day. Often the eggs are open to symbolise the empty tomb of Jesus. In Orthodox families children often crack hard-boiled eggs against each other saying 'Christ is risen'. Easter is not only a time to remember but also a time to experience and enjoy.

IN THE GLOSSARY

Anglican Church; Bible; Christmas; Easter; Holy Communion; Maundy Thursday; Orthodox Church; Paschal Candle; Priest; Resurrection; Roman Catholic Church; Vigil.

WHAT DO YOU KNOW?

1 a What do Christians celebrate on Easter Day?

b Easter is a 'moveable' festival. What does this mean?

c What is the Paschal Candle?

d What part does light play in the celebrations of Easter? Why?

e What is the Easter Vigil?

2 Imagine that you are present at an Easter Vigil in a Roman Catholic or Orthodox service for the first time. Write down ten words which might describe your impressions of the service.

3 It could be argued that light is the most powerful of all the Christian symbols. Why do you think that light is such a strong symbol? What does it suggest to you?

ASCENSION DAY AND PENTECOST

- **Many churches celebrate the ascension of Jesus into heaven at the end of his life on Ascension Day.**
- **All Christian churches celebrate the giving of the Holy Spirit to the early disciples of Jesus at Pentecost.**
- **Early converts were baptised at Pentecost wearing white clothes leading to the festival being called 'Whitsun'.**

Whilst neither Ascension Day nor Pentecost rank amongst the most important Church festivals they are still widely celebrated. When these two festivals are completed there are no more major festivals until the Christian Year starts again with Advent at the end of November.

A *Why does Ascension Day always fall on a Thursday?*

Ascension Day

Just 40 days after Easter Day some churches celebrate the ascension of Jesus into heaven at the end of his human life. As Easter Day is always a Sunday so Ascension Day always falls on a Thursday. The day is sometimes called Holy Thursday. Ascension Day is a 'holy day of obligation' for all Roman Catholics which means that they are expected to attend Mass on this day. Many Anglican churches also have a special Holy Communion to celebrate the reception of Jesus into heaven by God. The Paschal Candle which has been lit for every service in church since Easter Day is now finally extinguished. The story that began with the birth of Jesus has moved full circle through his death and resurrection to his return to God, the Father, in heaven.

Whitsun

Whitsun, or Pentecost as it is often called, follows ten days after Ascension Day. Pentecost is a Jewish festival which was being celebrated by the Jews in Jerusalem when the Holy Spirit was given by God to the early Christians. This event, called the 'Day of Pentecost', is described in Acts 2.1–12. Prior to this the disciples had huddled together behind closed doors afraid that the Roman soldiers would arrest them. Now, after receiving the Holy Spirit, they went out and fearlessly

***B** Why is the Holy Spirit usually pictured in the form of a dove?*

preached about Jesus in Jerusalem and the countries beyond.

As a result the Christian Church was born. We are told that 3,000 converts were added to the Church on the Day of Pentecost alone as a result of the preaching of Peter and John. Pentecost soon became a popular time for baptising the early converts to the faith. In this country those people who were baptised wore white clothes for the ceremony – to show that their sins had been forgiven by Jesus. Later Pentecost became known as 'White Sunday' or 'Whitsun'. This was a very appropriate time to baptise new converts since the Holy Spirit, given at Pentecost, had appeared to Jesus, in the form of a dove, when he had been baptised (Mark 1.1–11). You will often find a dove visible somewhere in a church. When the Holy Spirit was given to the first disciples he came to them as 'tongues of fire'. This is why the dominant colour in church, and in the clothes worn by priests, at Penetcost is red.

IN THE GLOSSARY

Advent; Ascension Day; Bible; Easter; Holy Communion; Holy Spirit; Jerusalem; Mass; Paschal Candle; Pentecost; Peter; Priest; Roman Catholic Church; Sunday; Whitsun.

WHAT DO YOU KNOW?

1 a How many days are there between Easter Day and Ascension Day?

b Ascension Day is a 'day of obligation' in the Catholic Church. What does this mean?

c What is lit in some churches for every service between Easter Day and Ascension Day?

d What is another name for Pentecost and why?

e What happened on the Day of Pentecost?

2 Ascension Day is only celebrated by a minority of churches – largely because Christians are uncertain about the ascension of Jesus into heaven. Why do you think this event causes problems for many Christians?

3 Can you work out why the Paschal Candle, which is kept alight in some churches for all services after Easter, is finally extinguished on Ascension Day?

4 Christian beliefs

THE CREEDS

- **Creeds were drawn up to distinguish between those who believed what the Church taught and those who did not.**
- **Creeds were used to teach new converts the meaning of the Christian faith before they were baptised.**
- **Two Creeds, the Nicene and the Apostles, have played an important part in Christian worship over the centuries.**

From its beginning the Church has drawn a line between people who hold acceptable beliefs and those who do not. People with unacceptable beliefs have been called 'heretics'. In the end these people have been expelled (excommunicated) from the Church and its worship.

A *This creed stands outside a church. The church has posted a list of its main beliefs so that everyone can see them. Why do you think they have done this?*

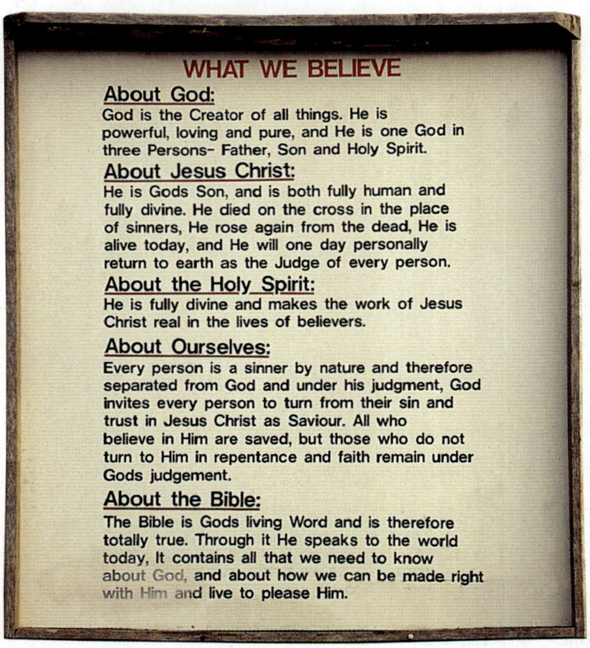

The Creeds

The Church needed a clear statement of belief to distinguish between those who were heretics and those who were not. This is where the Creeds came in. They also provided information to be taught to new Christians. These people needed a clear understanding of the Christian faith before they could be baptised. They could learn what the Creeds said about God, Jesus and the Holy Spirit off by heart

In 2,000 years there have only been two important Creeds which the Church has used widely in its worship. They are:

a The Nicene Creed. Emperor Constantine, the first Christian Roman Emperor, called a Council of all Christian bishops at Nicea in 325. The Creed that they produced has been the most widely used by the Church.

b The Apostles Creed. For a long time people thought that this Creed had come from the original apostles of Jesus. If so, it would have told us what the early

B This is one statement of belief found in both the Apostles and Nicene Creeds. Find out what other statements there are.

Christian Church had believed. As we now know, though, the Apostles Creed does not go back any earlier than the fourth century.

The Creeds and worship

These two Creeds still play a part in worship in the Anglican, Roman Catholic and Orthodox Churches. At some point in many services the people turn to face the altar and repeat the Creed together. This does not mean that each person believes everything in the Creed. The Creed is being used to express the unity of the people as Christians. They are saying that what unites them as Christians is more important than what divides them. This is why Anglicans, Roman Catholics and Orthodox Christians can all say the same Creed – even though they have many differences of belief.

The two Creeds move through all that is important in Christian belief – God creating the world; the birth of Jesus; the death of Jesus; the resurrection of Jesus and his return to the world from heaven. Other Christians also believe the same but they do not say the Creed in their services.

IN THE GLOSSARY

Altar; Anglican Church; Apostle; Apostles Creed; Creed; Nicene Creed; Orthodox Church; Roman Catholic Church.

WHAT DO YOU KNOW?

1 a What is a Creed?

b Why were Creeds drawn up in the early centuries of the Church?

c Which two Creeds have played an important part in Christian worship?

d When Christians face the altar and say the Creed together what are they expressing?

e What beliefs are in the Creed?

2 Imagine that you are an early convert to the Christian faith. You do not have a Christian background. What do you think you would find most difficult as you try to understand your new faith?

3 The Church has not drawn up a statement of its belief for centuries. Suggest why.

4 Christian beliefs

THE TRINITY

- **Christians believe in one God.**
- **The Christian God shows himself in three ways – as God the Father, God the Son and God the Holy Spirit.**
- **This Christian belief is called the Trinity.**

Some Christian beliefs are very difficult to understand and others are simply impossible! The Christian belief about the Trinity belongs to this second group. All that we can do is to try to explain what it means.

A *This banner brings together two members of the Trinity. What is it trying to say about them?*

Problems

The early Christians had a problem because almost all of them were Jews and they believed in the one God who created the heaven and the earth. These Christians, though, also believed that Jesus was God. The problem was complicated further because Christians believed that Jesus died on a cross. How could God possibly die? They also believed that the Holy Spirit was God. Did Christians believe in three Gods (tritheism) or in one God who took three different forms?

The Trinity

The early Christians were absolutely sure about one thing – they did not believe in three Gods. Their opponents might sometimes accuse them of this but it was never the belief of the Church. They believed that the one God shows himself in three different ways:

a **As God the Father.** God the Father made the world at the beginning of time and continues to look after it. This God made himself known to the Jews and led them out of slavery in Egypt towards their Promised Land of Israel. The story of God and the Jews is in the Old Testament.

b **As Jesus Christ (God, the Son).** Jesus came from heaven, was born to the Virgin Mary and lived in first-century Palestine. God was the father of Jesus. He was conceived in Mary's womb by the Holy Spirit. Jesus

B What are the problems in talking about God as a Trinity

did not have a human father or mother like every other human being – yet he was a real human being. After a short human life Jesus was put to death by the Romans and brought back to life by God. Having shown everyone how they should live Jesus left the earth and returned to God, his Father, in heaven. Christians expect Jesus to return to the earth at some time in the future to set up God's kingdom.

c **As the Holy Spirit.** God's love and power are working in the world today through the Holy Spirit. Jesus gave the Holy Spirit to the Church before he left the earth so that he could continue to show all that Jesus gave to the world.

The most well-known attempt to provide us with a 'picture' of the Trinity is that linked with the name of St Patrick. He showed the people he was teaching a shamrock. This has three leaves, perfectly joined together and yet it is a single leaf. Christians believe that God the Father, God the Son and God the Holy Spirit are different in the work they carry out. Yet they are perfectly united as one.

IN THE GLOSSARY

Bible; Holy Spirit; Trinity; Virgin Mary.

WHAT DO YOU KNOW?

1 a **What do Jews believe about God?**
b **What is the Trinity?**
c **What do Christians believe about Jesus?**
d **What do Christians believe about the Holy Spirit?**
e **How did St Patrick use the shamrock to teach others about the Trinity?**

2 **Can you think of any other 'picture' which Christians might use today to illustrate the Trinity to make it clearer to people? Think of objects which begin with the prefix 'tri'.**

3 **Do you think that God is involved in some way with the world in which we live today? The Christian belief in the Trinity suggests that he is. If so, can you suggest one way in which God is involved.**

GOD, THE FATHER

- **Christians believe that God is beyond human understanding – yet human beings can be friends with God.**
- **God is a mystery.**
- **God is a Spirit.**

Christians believe in one God. Because this one God is so great human beings can never know or understand him fully. Christians believe, however, that it is possible to know God as a friend. Jesus often spoke about God. His favourite term to describe God was as his 'Father' and this is the way he encouraged his followers to think of God. The prayer that Jesus taught his followers to use, the Lord's Prayer, begins with the words 'Our Father who art in heaven hallowed be thy name…' (Matthew 6.9)

A What do you think someone might learn about God by watching a father with his baby?

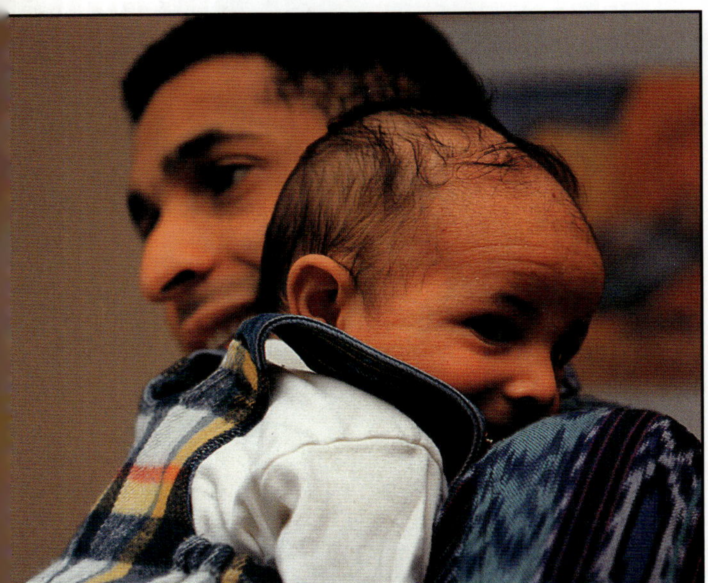

To Christians God is:

a A Mystery – beyond all human understanding. The Bible makes it clear that God has always existed – he was not created. God has no beginning – and he does not have an end. He is outside time and yet he is present in the world and he cares about the creatures that he has made. Human beings can see the result of God's activity in the world but they cannot see God. In the Old Testament it was believed that if anyone saw God he would die instantly. God was always covered with a cloud. Behind all life there is mystery and Christians believe that this mystery is God.

Christian worship tries to express this mystery. The hymns and prayers express the belief that people can enter into a relationship with God, a real friendship. Yet human beings can never take this relationship for granted. They must always keep their distance from God. In fact, there is always an immense distance between God and creation. This distance is symbolised in a church by the altar. During worship the priest presents the worship of the people to God but they cannot draw any closer because of their sins. This is expressed most clearly in the Orthodox Holy Liturgy where the people can only catch a glimpse of the altar behind the iconostasis during the service.

B Do you think that God is the creator of all the love in the world?

b A Spirit. Jesus called God a Spirit as if that answered all questions but, of course, it doesn't. God is a Spirit who is everywhere at the same time and never just in the one place. We can only guess at what this might mean. It seems to suggest that God perfectly shows the all-important 'spiritual' qualities, such as love, peace and joy, to everyone. These qualities are found everywhere. Such qualities come from God and if human beings ever experience them then it is because God has given them as gifts to be freely received. They can never be deserved or earned.

c The Creator. There are two stories in the Bible about how everything in the world began – found in Genesis 1 and 2. If you cannot remember how they differ from each other then refresh your memory by reading them through. Remember one thing – you are not reading about how life really began. You are reading a piece of poetry to explain that God was there working on creation from the very beginning.

IN THE GLOSSARY

Altar; Bible; Lord's Prayer.

WHAT DO YOU KNOW?

1 a What term did Jesus use to describe God?

b How does Christian worship try to explain the mystery which is God?

c What does the altar in a church express?

d What does it mean to speak of God as a Spirit?

e In which prayer do Christians express their belief in God, their Father?

2 Find a copy of the Nicene or Apostles Creed. Make a list of all the statements which you can find in the Creed about God.

3 What do you think Jesus really meant when he called God his Father? Many people have misunderstood his words. What do you think he had in mind? Could some people find it unhelpful to speak of God in this way? If so, why?

4 Christian beliefs

JESUS, GOD'S SON

- **Jesus Christ is the focus of Christian worship.**
- **Christians believe that Jesus is God, a part of the Trinity.**
- **Whilst on earth Jesus was both fully God and totally human.**

Christian worship centres around Jesus, the Son of God. It is directed to God through Jesus. Christians believe that Jesus came to show the people what God is like. Without Jesus people would know little about God. The four Gospels in the New Testament tell us all that we need to know about Jesus. They show him to have been a special teacher, friend, healer and Saviour.

A What do you think many people found attractive about the life of Jesus?

Jesus, the Son of God

The Gospels express how the early Christians felt about Jesus and what they believed about him. From the Gospels we discover four important pieces of information about Jesus:

a Jesus is God. Christians believe that Jesus is part of the Trinity along with God the Father and the Holy Spirit. Jesus is that part of the Trinity who left heaven and came to earth to be born as a baby in a stable in Bethlehem. This event is known to Christians as the 'Incarnation' and is celebrated each year in the festival of Christmas.

Christians believe that Jesus was fully God and fully human. Obviously he did not act like God when he was on earth. He suffered and died and Christians have struggled with this for 2,000 years. From time to time, though, we can glimpse in the Gospels the Christian belief that Jesus was divine. One example is the birth of Jesus where two Gospels, Matthew and Luke, insist that Jesus was not conceived like any other baby. His conception and birth were a miracle. Mary, his mother, was a virgin when Jesus was conceived and born.

b Jesus lived a normal human life on earth. Before Jesus emerged as a teacher and miracle worker he was brought up like any other Jewish boy. At the age of 30 he responded to the call of God to be a travelling preacher telling the people that God's

B What do the four Gospels tell us about Jesus?

kingdom was beginning on earth. Jesus gathered a group of followers around him and began to teach so they could continue his work when he left the earth.

c **Jesus was put to death by his enemies.** The Apostles Creed says: 'He suffered under Pontius Pilate, was crucified, died and was buried.' Two days later Christians believe that Jesus was brought back to life by God. These two events, his death and resurrection, are celebrated by Christians throughout the world on Good Friday and Easter Day. Reminders of this death in the form of crosses and crucifixes are found in most churches.

d **Jesus left the earth and returned to his Father in heaven.** This event is known as the Ascension and is celebrated by some churches each year on Ascension Day. As Jesus left his disciples he gave them the promise that he would return to the earth sometime in the future. Christians are still waiting for the Second Coming of Christ.

IN THE GLOSSARY

Apostles Creed; Ascension Day; Christmas; Crucifix; Easter; Good Friday; Gospel; Incarnation; New Testament; Second Coming; Trinity; Virgin Mary.

WHAT DO YOU KNOW?

1 a Where do Christians find all that they need to know about Jesus?

b What is the Incarnation?

c What do Christians believe was special, and unique, about the birth of Jesus?

d Which two very important events are celebrated by Christians on Good Friday and Easter Day?

e What do Christians believe about Jesus now that he has ascended to his Father in heaven?

2 Imagine that you are one of the disciples of Jesus. At the end of Jesus' earthly life you look back over his time on the earth. You are trying to understand just who Jesus was. What do you think your assessment of Jesus might have been?

3 Many people find different aspects of the life of Jesus difficult to understand, or accept. Is there anything about Jesus that causes you particular problems?

4 Christian beliefs

THE DEATH AND RESURRECTION OF JESUS

- **The death and resurrection of Jesus are the two most important events in the Gospels for all Christians.**
- **Christians believe that Jesus died so that the sins of the whole world might be forgiven.**
- **The resurrection of Jesus showed that God had accepted his death and that everyone who believes can look forward to eternal life.**

There are two events in the life of Jesus which are far more important than any others in the Gospels. They form the foundation on which everything else in the Christian faith stands. They are:

a Jesus' death on a cross in Jerusalem.

b Jesus' return to life two days later.

A *How did the death of Jesus bring God and human beings together?*

The death of Jesus

Christians believe that Jesus was a unique person. In particular, he was the God who became a human being. Because he was unique his death was truly extraordinary – and very special. In church each worshipper is surrounded by reminders of this death. Jesus did not die because he was guilty of committing any crime. Christians believe that Jesus lived a faultless life. He was put to death because the religious leaders of the time persuaded the Roman authorities that he was a threat to them.

Yet, Christians have always believed that the death of Jesus was far more than a simple miscarriage of justice. This death, in a small Eastern country has had a tremendous effect on history. Christians use the word 'atonement' to describe what Jesus brought about by his death. The word 'atonement' means to put everything right after something has gone wrong. As Jesus did not sin at any time during his earthly life so he could not have been suffering because of his own sins. Jesus died because of the sins of the whole world. These sins separated God and the human race but, by his death, Jesus brought them together – he made them 'at-one'.

B *How was the resurrection of Jesus important to Christians?*

Through their worship Christians preach the Gospel – the Good News. The good news of the Christian faith is that everyone can have their sins forgiven. People can enter into a new friendship with God. Without this forgiveness worship of God would be impossible. Through it, though, Christians can begin to enjoy the kind of life which stretches beyond the end of time into eternity.

The resurrection of Jesus

Christians believe that shortly after dying Jesus was brought back to life by God. No one knows just what happened in the tomb of Jesus 2,000 years ago and the Gospels certainly do not tell us how Jesus was brought back to life. They do agree, however, that we are dealing with a unique event. Paul expressed his own belief that if Jesus had not risen from the dead then the whole Christian faith would be meaningless. Jesus' resurrection is extremely important for all Christians. It is the foundation on which everything else is built.

IN THE GLOSSARY

Atonement; Easter; Gospel; Jerusalem; Paul.

WHAT DO YOU KNOW?

1 a **Which are the two most important events in the life of Jesus for all Christians?**
b **Why did Jesus die?**
c **What does the word 'Atonement' mean?**
d **What is the 'Good News' that the Christian Church preaches?**
e **Why is the resurrection of Jesus very important for all Christians?**

2 **Imagine that you are a young Christian trying to explain to a friend why the death of Jesus is so important to you. What would you say?**

3 **Why do you think it is important for Christians to believe that the death and resurrection of Jesus were unique (never-to-be-repeated) events?**

4 Christian beliefs

THE HOLY SPIRIT

- **Christians believe that the Holy Spirit is the third member of the Trinity.**
- **Jesus gave the Holy Spirit to the Church to be its Comforter and Guide in his absence.**
- **Many Christians today believe that the Holy Spirit's power and gifts should be experienced in the Church.**

Christians believe that the Holy Spirit is the third member of the Trinity. The Holy Spirit is the power of God in the world today. Before he left the earth Jesus promised that he would give the Holy Spirit to his followers. This took place on the Day of Pentecost. You can read about this event for yourself in Acts 2.1–12.

The Holy Spirit

Christians believe that the Holy Spirit has always been active in the world. In the story of God creating the world we are told that the Spirit of God turned a vast tract of darkness and wasteland into a beautiful world. The Spirit then crops up many times as God's agent in the world throughout the Old Testament. Later Mary is told by the Angel Gabriel that the Holy Spirit would come upon her and she would conceive Jesus, the Son of God. The conception and birth of Jesus would be truly unique.

John the Baptist announced that when Jesus, the Messiah, came he would baptise the people with the Holy Spirit rather than with water – as John had been doing. When Jesus himself came to be baptised we are told that the Holy Spirit descended on him like a dove. Jesus often spoke with his disciples about the Holy Spirit who would replace him as their constant guide. He called the Holy Spirit the 'Comforter' or 'Guide'.

The Holy Spirit today

Many Christians believe that the power of the Holy Spirit can be experienced by Christians in the Church

A *What did Jesus tell his disciples had to take place before they could be given the Holy Spirit?*

B Why was a dove a particularly good symbol for the Holy Spirit?

today. Those who believe that the Holy Spirit can be experienced directly are called Pentecostal or Charismatic Christians. They talk about people being 'baptised in the Spirit' or 'filled with the Spirit'. As a result there are Christians who are able to:

a Speak and pray to God in a language that they do not understand. People who have this 'gift' speak of the great joy that this brings to their worship as they are able to praise God properly.

b Heal people who are ill. Healing is a gift which is used in many branches of the Church and is often accompanied by anointing sick people with oil – a practice known and used in the New Testament. This is obviously following in the footsteps of Jesus who healed many people.

c Cast demons out of people who are demon-possessed. Some Christians believe that much illness and depression are caused by a person being possessed by evil powers. These evil powers come from Satan, the Devil.

IN THE GLOSSARY
Holy Spirit; Satan; Trinity.

WHAT DO YOU KNOW?

1 a When do Christians believe that the Holy Spirit was given to the Church?
b How was the Spirit involved when God created the world?
c What was the involvement of the Spirit of God in the conception and birth of Jesus?
d How was the baptism of Jesus different from that offered by John the Baptist?
e Who are Pentecostal Christians and what do they believe?

2 The Holy Spirit has been called 'the least known member of the Trinity'. Why do you think that many Christians find it difficult to understand the work that the Holy Spirit does?

3 Pentecostal and Charismatic Christians form the quickest growing group in the Christian Church. These churches are expanding at a time when other Churches are losing members quickly. Can you suggest any reason for this?

4 Christian beliefs

THE VIRGIN MARY

- **Roman Catholic and Orthodox Christians hold the Virgin Mary in the greatest possible respect.**
- **Some Christians believe that Mary was born without sin and went straight to heaven at the end of her life.**
- **Roman Catholics believe that Mary intercedes with God for them and helps them as they pray.**

All Roman Catholic churches have a statue of the Virgin Mary. There are usually votive candles in front of the statue which people light as they enter church. Mary will also be found on many of the icons which play a very important part in Orthodox worship. To Catholics she is 'Our Lady' as well as the 'Mother of God' showing that she gave birth to Jesus, the Son of God. A favourite Orthodox description of Mary is as 'Theotokos' (Mother of God). Protestant Churches respect Mary as the mother of Jesus, the Saviour, but they do not believe that she was more than an ordinary human being.

***A** What do Catholics mean when they talk about the 'Immaculate Conception' of the Virgin Mary?*

Mary, an example to all

When Mary was told by an angel in Luke's Gospel that she was going to give birth to Jesus, God's Son, she was initially very apprehensive. This was hardly surprising but she soon came to accept the will of God – even though she was young and unmarried. She accepted that the father of her child would not be Joseph, to whom she was engaged, but the Holy Spirit. To Roman Catholic and Orthodox Christians this makes Mary the perfect example for others to follow – an example of humility and obedience. Every Christian should follow in her footsteps and show the same accepting obedience of the will of God.

Both the Roman Catholic and the Orthodox Churches believe the same things about the Virgin Mary, as they call her. They believe that:

a Mary was born sinless. Every other human being is

B *What do Catholics mean when they talk about the 'Assumption of the Virgin Mary'?*

born with a tendency to sin (called 'Original Sin') but Mary was different ('The Immaculate Conception').

b Mary was chosen by God to bear his Son, Jesus.

c Mary gave birth to Jesus without any human father being involved in his conception ('The Virgin Birth').

d Mary went straight to heaven at the end of her life without dying ('The Assumption of the Virgin Mary').

There are many icons in Orthodox churches which show Mary, usually with the baby Jesus in her arms. These churches believe that she is in heaven praying for the souls of those who are still alive on earth. They believe that Mary is able to represent them before God. Many Roman Catholic and Orthodox prayers are directed to Mary who can then 'interceed' (plead) for them with God. Having lit a votive candle in front of Mary's statue a prayer is offered to her. The Church shows how grateful it is for the work that Mary does by dedicating more than one festival each year to her memory.

IN THE GLOSSARY

Holy Spirit; Icon; Original Sin; Orthodox Church; Roman Catholic Church; Virgin Birth; Virgin Mary.

WHAT DO YOU KNOW?

1 a What will you usually find in front of a statue of the Virgin Mary in a Roman Catholic church?

b What are two beliefs which Roman Catholic and Orthodox Christians hold about the Virgin Mary?

c What is the belief of Protestants about the Virgin Mary?

d What kind of example does Mary set to Christians?

e Why is Mary such an important object of devotion for Roman Catholics?

2 Why do you think that Roman Catholics find it helpful to pray in front of a statue of the Virgin Mary and Orthodox believers in front of an icon?

3 Roman Catholic and Orthodox Christians believe that Mary went straight to heaven at the end of her life. What do you think this belief is trying to say about Mary?

GLOSSARY

A

Abbot Monk who is leader of a monastery.

Absolution Pronouncement by priest of the forgiveness of sins.

Advent Season in Christian Year leading up to Christmas.

Altar Table in church where Holy Communion is conducted.

Anglican Church Churches based on the teachings of the Church of England.

Apostle Name given to disciples after Jesus left the earth.

Apostles Creed An important early statement of Christian belief.

Ascension Day Day on which some Christians celebrate the ascension of Jesus into heaven.

Ash Wednesday The first day of Lent.

Atonement Belief that Jesus brought together God and the human race by his death.

B

Baptism Ceremony of washing away of sins by the sprinkling of water.

Baptist Church Nonconformist Church which believes in the baptism of adults.

Believer's baptism Ceremony in Baptist Church in which only adult believers are baptised.

Bible The holy book of Christians.

Bishop Senior priest in the Anglican and Roman Catholic Churches.

Bishop of Rome Title given to the Pope.

Breaking of Bread Title used in many Nonconformist churches for Holy Communion.

C

Cathedral Church in which the bishop of a diocese conducts many of the services.

Celibacy The rule in the Roman Catholic Church that its priests are not allowed to marry.

Chrismation The service in the Orthodox Church in which a baby is baptised and confirmed at the same time.

Christmas The Christian festival that celebrates the birth of Jesus.

Church of England The most important Church in England, led by the Archbishop of Canterbury.

Citadel The building in which members of the Salvation Army worship.

Confirmation The service in an Anglican and Roman Catholic church in which a person confirms their baptismal vows.

Convent The place in which a community of nuns live.

Creed An old statement of belief.

Crib A model representing the scene of Christ's birth.

Crucifix Small cross found in many churches holding the figure of Jesus.

Curate An assistant priest.

D

Devil The source of all evil, also known as Satan.

Diocese The area over which a bishop presides.

E

Easter Day The day on which Christians celebrate the resurrection of Jesus from the dead.

Epiphany The festival at which Christians celebrate the visit of the Wise Men to the infant Jesus.

Epistles Letters in the New Testament, written by followers of Jesus.

Eucharist 'Thanksgiving', the name often used in Anglican churches for Holy Communion.

F

Fasting The old practice of going without food for a time to dedicate oneself to prayer.

Font Stone receptacle in many churches holding water for infant baptism.

G

Good Friday The day on which Christians remember the death of Jesus.

Gospel One of four books in the New Testament which tell the story of Jesus.

H

Hail Mary An important Roman Catholic prayer addressed to the Virgin Mary.

Holy Communion The most important act of Christian worship at which people eat bread and drink wine to remember the death of Jesus.

Holy Liturgy Name given in the Orthodox Church to Holy Communion.

Holy Orders Name given to the situation of those priests who have been ordained.

Holy Spirit The third member of the Christian Trinity.

Holy Week Time of Christian Year running from Palm Sunday to Good Friday.

House Church A church that meets in the houses of its members.

Hymn A song used in Christian worship.

I

Icon A picture used widely in Orthodox worship.

Iconostasis Screen at front of Orthodox Church, containing icons.

Incarnation Christian belief that Jesus, the Son of God, was born as a human being.

Infant baptism The practice followed in most churches of baptising babies.

J

Jerusalem City at the centre of the Jewish faith, place where Jesus was crucified.

L

Last Supper The last meal that Jesus ate with his disciples, pattern for Holy Communion.

Lectern Platform at the front of a church on which a Bible stands.

Lent The time of preparation leading up to the celebration of Easter.

Liturgy Any set pattern for a service in church.

Lord's Prayer The prayer that Jesus taught his disciples to use, used in most Christian services.

Lord's Supper Name given to Holy Communion in many Nonconformist churches.

M

Mass The name given to the service of Holy Communion in a Roman Catholic church.

Maundy Thursday The day before Good Friday, on which Christians remember the Last Supper.

Meditation A largely silent form of praying.

Meeting house The building in which Quakers meet for worship.

Mercy seat Platform at the front of Salvation Army citadel where people kneel to ask for God's forgiveness.

Messiah The leader that Jews expected God to send to them, Christians believe that Jesus was the Messiah.

Methodist Church Nonconformist Church based on the teaching of John Wesley in the eighteenth century.

Minister The leader of worship in a Nonconformist church.

Monastery The building in which monks live and worship.

Monk Someone who belongs to a monastic order.

Mother Superior The leader of a convent.

N

Nave The gangway down the middle of most churches.

New Testament The second part of the Bible, the part that contains the story of Jesus.

Nicene Creed One of the most important statements of Christian belief

Nonconformist Church A Church which is not Anglican, Roman Catholic or Orthodox.

Nun A woman who belongs to a monastic order.

O

Old Testament The first part of the Bible, contains the books of the Jewish Scriptures

Ordination The service at which men and women become priests, gives them the authority to give the sacraments.

Original Sin The sin committed by the first man and woman in the Garden of Eden.

Orthodox Church The Church, mainly Eastern which places a great emphasis on ceremony.

P

Palm Sunday The day on which Christians remember the entry of Jesus into Jerusalem on a donkey, the first day of Holy Week.

Paschal Candle Candle lit on Easter Day, lit in all church services until Ascension Day.

Passover The most important festival in the Jewish calendar. It commemorates the exodus of the Jews from slavery in Egypt.

Paul The main leader of the early Christian Church.

Penance Penalty carried out by Roman Catholics to show their sincerity in seeking God's forgiveness for sins.

Pentecost The Christian festival celebrating the giving of the Holy Spirit to the first disciples, also known as Whitsun.

Peter A disciple of Jesus, the first leader of the Early Church.

Pope Leader of Roman Catholic Church, believed to be successor of St Peter.

Prayer book A book in some Churches that contains the services.

Priest Man, or woman in some Churches, who can take services and give the sacraments.

Protestant Person who belongs to a Church which is neither Roman Catholic nor Orthodox.

Psalm A Jewish song designed to be used in worship.

Pulpit Platform in church from which a sermon is delivered.

Purgatory The place where Roman Catholics believe most people spend time being prepared for heaven.

Q

Quakers A group formed in the seventeenth century, most of its worship services are spent in silence.

R

Reconciliation Roman Catholic sacrament, offering forgiveness of sins.

Resurrection The raising of Jesus from the dead.

Roman Catholic Church The largest Christian Church, led by the Pope.

Rood screen Screen erected in many churches to separate the altar from the people, almost all of them have now been removed.

Rosary Special string of beads, used by many Roman Catholics as an aid to prayer.

Royal doors The doors in the middle of the iconostasis in an Orthodox church.

S

Sacrament A special service through which a blessing from God is received.

Saint Someone who is known for the holiness of their life.

Salvation Army Nonconformist Church, formed in the nineteenth century, wears a distinctive uniform.

Satan The source of all evil in the world, also known as the Devil.

Second Coming The Christian belief that Jesus will come to the earth for a second time.

Sermon The part of a service when the priest, or someone else, explains a part of the Bible.

Shrove Tuesday The day before Lent begins on Ash Wednesday.

Sunday The day on which most Christians try to worship together in church.

Synoptic Gospels Three of the four Gospels – Matthew, Mark and Luke – which present a similar picture of the life of Jesus.

T

Ten Commandments The ten laws given to Moses by God in the Old Testament.

Transubstantiation The belief of the Roman Catholic Church that in the Mass the bread and wine become the actual body and blood of Christ.

Trinity The Christian belief in God.

U

United Reformed Church A Nonconformist Church.

V

Viaticum 'Food for the Journey', the last Holy Communion given by a Roman Catholic priest before a person dies.

Vicar An Anglican priest who is responsible for one, or more, churches.

Vigil A service at which people 'watch' with Jesus in the last few hours of his life on Good Friday.

Virgin Birth The Christian teaching that Mary conceived Jesus through the Holy Spirit without having had sexual intercourse.

Virgin Mary The mother of Jesus, the object of devotion for Roman Catholic and Orthodox believers.

Vocation 'Calling', the calling of someone to serve God as a priest, monk or nun.

W

Whitsun 'White Sunday', otherwise known as Pentecost.